RESEARCH REPORT

Hypoxic Air Venting for Protection of Heritage

Author

Geir Jensen, COWI AS, Norway

Contributing Authors

Lic. Eng. Jan G. Holmberg, KTH Building Sciences, Sweden

Dr. Eng. Arne Gussiås, COWI AS, Norway

Cand. Scient. Marianne Melgård, COWI AS, Norway

Ola Thomas Fjerdingen, COWI AS, Norway

Jointly Published by

Riksantikvaren the Norwegian Directorate for Cultural Heritage

Historic Scotland: Technical Conservation, Research and Education Group

in Support of

COST – the European CO-operation in the field of Scientific and Technical Research –
Action C17 Built Heritage: Fire Loss to Historic Buildings

ISBN 82-7574-037-1

CONTENTS

EXECUTIVE SUMMARY 3

DEFINITIONS 5

1 HYPOXIC AIR FIRE PREVENTION 6
   1.1 Hypoxic air 6
   1.2 Inerting methods 8
   1.3 Application potential 9
   1.4 Hypoxic air versus other fire protection alternatives 11

2 HYPOXIC AIR SYSTEM DESIGNS 12
   2.1 Nitrogen feed 12
   2.2 Hypoxic air venting 12
   2.3 Inerting on demand 14

3 REGULATION, STANDARDS AND AVAILABILITY 15
   3.1 Regulation bodies 15
   3.2 Standards, approval bodies, installation guidelines 15
   3.3 Market availability 16

4 IMPLICATIONS FOR HERITAGE 17
   4.1 Potential applications 17
   4.2 Fire prevention 17
   4.3 Reduced degradation of artefacts 17
   4.4 Reduced degradation of building structure and fabric 23
   4.5 Health and safety 24
   4.6 Secondary damage 31
   4.7 Operating modes 31
   4.8 Installation 32
   4.9 Maintenance, energy consumption and lifetime cost 36
   4.10 Challenges in need of research 36

5 CASE STUDIES 37
   5.1 Introduction 37
   5.2 Arezzo Public Library (Italy) 38
   5.3 Historic Scotland Stenhouse Conservation Centre (Scotland) ...44
   5.4 Linnékuben (Sweden) 48
   5.5 Trøndelag Folk Museum (Norway) 51

6 CONCLUSIONS 60

REFERENCES 64

APPENDICES

A Comments on a key reference: *Fire Prevention and Health
   Assessment in Hypoxic Environment* (Master Thesis of Berg and
   Lindgren. Lund University).[13] 69
B Published information by manufacturers 71

EXECUTIVE SUMMARY

A novel technique to protect heritage buildings and artefacts from fire and degradation has been evaluated.

Inert air, referred to as hypoxic air (reduced oxygen concentration), comprises slightly altered concentrations of components of air. Typically 5% of the oxygen content is substituted by nitrogen. Inert air has predetermined oxygen level and safely vents the space to be protected continuously. Inert air is safe to breathe, but prevents fire ignition in common materials. Inert air replaces the use of inert gases.

The exploration of inert air for fire protection is recent, and several milestones have been passed in quick succession over the past ten years. Three years ago, the concept of premixed hypoxic air feed into the protected room superseded the technique of nitrogen feed into the room until hypoxic air is established, and made the inert air option safer, simpler and less expensive. A rush of research and development for various applications are being made, such as vital rooms for telecommunication. The United States Federal Aviation Administration has proposed regulation to retrofit all commercial airplanes with hypoxic ventilation for fuel tanks. The potential benefits to heritage are many.

Inert air is generated by simple and reliable units that fit into air conditioning plants, or mobile autonomous units are located in or adjacent to at rooms to be protected.

Implementation issues on fire safety, health, cost, reliability, maintenance and impact on artefacts and fabrics have been evaluated. A list of hypotheses which stated potential benefits and drawbacks for heritage applications was analysed.

Fire protection of heritage has always been challenging. Fires do irreversible damage before they are extinguished and often firefighting agents cause secondary damage. Extinguishing equipment is often aesthetically obtrusive and may inflict damage to the building fabric or décor. Unintentional activations and routine maintenance may also damage artefacts, décor and fabric.

Inert air venting is found to be remarkably promising for heritage applications. Inert air prevents ignition, initial smoke and fire spread. Storage rooms, laboratories and exhibitions may be protected, with sizes ranging from small closets to large volumes. Public spaces could be treated in the same way as aircraft cabins where similar conditions pertain by not allowing individuals with predispositions for disease in hypoxic air to enter.

Pipes, nozzles or equipment in the protected rooms are generally not required. No room fans, room sensors, detection nor activation systems are required. The inert air is continuously generated on site, thus a minimum of space is required. Generators couple to the building air conditioning system or to inlet air ducts. Fully reversible mobile units may be located in the rooms. Unlike with gas extinguishing systems, no reservoirs run empty or require refilling.

It is shown that inert air venting has potential to avoid invasive installations. Both for single room and multiple room protection various designs allow for virtually no physical, aesthetic or irreversible invasions at all. There is virtually no risk of secondary damage, environmental or corrosive issues. The inert air may positively contribute to the diminishing of normal deterioration of organic and non organic objects as well as décor.

A challenge of implementing inert air systems is to optimize energy cost, which depends strongly on air exchange rate and air leakage. Compressors must be located or encapsulated to reduce noise. Analysis must be done to ensure that any special substance which may burn at low oxygen level are taken care of by other measures as with any inert gas extinguishing system, or by incorporating an inert air suppression-mode option.

Where inert air in prevention mode becomes impractical due to either access control of public areas or high energy consumption, inert air may be applied in suppression mode. In suppression mode a reservoir of inert air is dumped on demand, when prompted by fire detection; the system thereafter running for continuous protection. Suppression mode may involve inert air of lower oxygen concentration than the preventive mode, and people should evacuate - but the inert air is still safe to occupy for most people, even for extended periods.

Inert air venting systems for either prevention or suppression may not, by their inherent design, incidentally dump dangerous concentration of nitrogen or other substance. Systems produce or store safe inert air and fail-safe mode is pure air.

Some national code limits on oxygen level for confined enclosures in buildings may require special permit, or management measures such as control of staff or public areas to prevent access by individuals predisposed to heart disease etc.

In order to optimize inert air venting in the future, research should be done to further determine fire heat and smoke retarding effects, or damage per minute rates, in hypoxic air. Also, effects on smouldering fires should be investigated. Once cleared, there is a probability that the oxygen level may be increased further in some heritage applications.

Four case study examples demonstrate that a range of buildings may be well protected by properly designed continuous inert air systems. The Arezzo Public Library building and the Stenhouse building computer room offer moderate challenges in incorporating the installation. The Linné Building and the Arezzo Public Library building offer the most irreplaceable cultural values and should gain the most of benefits from inert air systems. The Trøndelag Folk Museum offers the least challenges and lends itself to cost-efficient installations.

More than 50 installations using inert air by the nitrogen feed principle are by now reported installed in Europe. Full coverage by the inert air venting principle is currently planned for two new public libraries in the Middle East.

DEFINITIONS OF TERMS & ACRONYMS USED

Anoxic Oxygenless. Anoxia: Of such severity as to result in permanent damage.

Hypobaric Pertaining to pressure of ambient gases below sea-level normal (>760 mmHg)

Hypoxia A reduction in the amount of oxygen available for tissue respiration.

Hypoxic The partial pressure of oxygen is lower than at sea level

Hypoxic environment Constant reduced oxygen concentration in an enclosure where a stable atmosphere can be maintained. In this context, in order to prevent fires. Another objective may be exercising for improved health.

Hypoxic air venting Generators provide precise premix of *hypoxic air* which substitutes the inflow of air to closets, rooms or large buildings. These provide uniform hypoxic air at all times without gas sensor feedback from room. Alternate expression: "*inert air venting*".

Inert air Air that is breathable, yet prevents ignition and retards combustion of common materials.

Inert air venting Alternate expression for "*hypoxic air venting*".

Inert gas Any of a group of rare gases that include helium, neon, argon, krypton, xenon, and sometimes radon and that exhibit great stability and extremely low reaction rates. Automatic suppression systems apply high concentration of inert gas or gas blends, and do not aim for sustained occupation, as do inert air venting or nitrogen feed.

Nitrogen A gaseous element which makes up approximately 80% of the earth's atmosphere. Nitrogen is relatively inert and does not support either combustion or life. Nitrogen is usually found in the molecular N_2 form

Nitrogen feed Nitrogen feed (to create hypoxic air in a room) resembles "gas flooding" concepts by which a gas extinguishant is fed into a room until a prescribed concentration is met. Although, in this context the concentration is low (hypoxic) and feeding continuous. Feedback by gas sensors in the room adjust the amount of nitrogen feed to keep the concentration as uniform as possible.

Normobaric Denoting a barometric pressure equivalent to sea- level pressure (760 mmHg)

Normoxic The partial pressure of oxygen corresponds to the pressure at sea level.

Oxidation Originally, oxidation meant a chemical reaction in which O_2 combines with another substance. The usage of the word has been broadened to include any reaction in which electrons are transferred. The substance which gains electrons is the oxidising agent.

Oxygen A gaseous element which makes up approximately 20% of the earth's atmosphere. It is usually found in the molecular form. O_2 is the most abundant element on earth.

Partial pressure of oxygen The partial pressure of oxygen is determined by the baromeric pressure. At sea level, the barometric pressure is 760 mmHg, and O_2 makes up 20.946 % of inspired air. At sea level O_2 exerts a partial pressure of about 159 mmHg (760x0.20946)

Pyrolysis The chemical degradation of a substance by the action of heat, in the presence or absence of O_2. Sometimes used to refer to a stage of fire before flaming combustion has occurred.

Total flooding The act and manner of discharging an agent for the purpose of achieving a specified minimum agent concentration throughout a hazard volume.

1 HYPOXIC AIR FOR FIRE PREVENTION

1.1 Hypoxic Air

Normal air is made up of a mixture of oxygen and nitrogen together with small quantities of other elements. Within this mix oxygen is a critical element which supports both life and combustion. Air that has had the relative concentrations of its constituent elements altered to reduce the oxygen content is called hypoxic air, or simply inert air, and can be created for enclosed spaces on site using specialised equipment. When produced via a continuous inerting system to give closely controlled predetermined oxygen concentrations, an atmosphere can be maintained with enough oxygen to enable humans to breathe but with insufficient oxygen for common materials to ignite or burn.

The hypoxic air generator may be part of the air conditioning system, and the spaces or complete building covered is thus provided with conditioned air in terms of fire safety as well as mere humidity and temperature. Generators typically add about 5% of nitrogen while removing 5% of oxygen to provide a continuous fire preventing environment in spaces for long term occupation.

Hypoxic air may alternatively be used as an extinguishing medium to provide a "suppression mode" of operation. Premixed hypoxic air is then released following detection of fire. The suppression mode requires personnel to evacuate as a precaution within 2 minutes, as with conventional inert gas extinguishing systems.

A NORMAL AIR VERSUS INERT AIR FOR PREVENTION

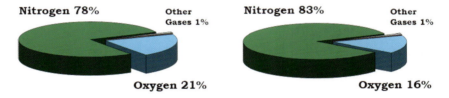

B NORMAL AIR VERSUS INERT AIR FOR SUPPRESSION

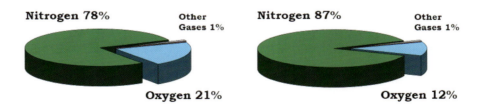

Figure 1: Air (left) and inert air (hypoxic air) (right) (illustration based on FirePASS[20]). The oxygen level of inert air for fire prevention is typically 15 to 16 %, and for suppression 10-12%[24].

The preventive and suppression modes operate with 15-16% and 10-12% concentration of oxygen respectively. The human body function well in the range of 15-21 % oxygen, consistent with altitudes of human inhabitation. Mexico City inhabitants live in about 15.5% of oxygen concentration, while aircraft staff and passengers experience 15.5-17.4%. In the Biosphere 2 research project (Walford) a variety of young and old persons lived for an extended time period in 14.2% of oxygen concentration with minor transient side effects only.

The concept of hypoxic air venting in this context is very simple, yet discovered recently: During research on hypoxic air systems it was discovered that the processes of ignition and combustion in an inert air (hypoxic) environment at sea level (normobaric, hypoxic environment) are far different from the ignition and combustion process that occur at a high altitude environment (hypobaric natural environment) with the same partial pressure of oxygen. See figure 1.

This surprising observation lead to an obvious question: Why do two environments for occupation which contain the same number of oxygen molecules per specific volume affect the processes of ignition and combustion so differently?

For detailed descriptions of inert air interactions with the human respiratory system and with the combustion process, see references Lund[13], Kotliar[21-30, 13]. For a summary explanation, refer to figures 2 and 3:

The human respiratory system is hardly affected by oxygen concentration levels from 15 to 21%, as is evident from populations at sea levels and at mountain altitudes concentrations equivalent to 15%, down to 12% are easily tolerated by local inhabitants. Access to oxygen molecules by our respiratory system is not affected by the content of added nitrogen in inert air at sea levels.

Combustion, however, is affected by the added nitrogen of inert air. The increased number of nitrogen molecules effectively block combustion processes from accessing oxygen molecules readily enough to sustain combustion.

The way inert air affects the human body and the flame is illustrated in figure 3. The health effects are further covered in chapter 4.5 and respective references.

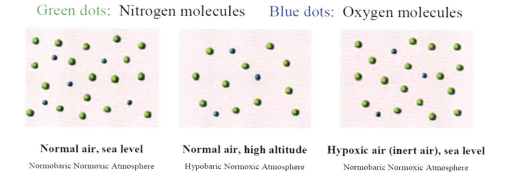

Green dots: Nitrogen molecules   Blue dots: Oxygen molecules

Normal air, sea level   **Normal air, high altitude**   **Hypoxic air (inert air), sea level**
Normobaric Normoxic Atmosphere   Hypobaric Normoxic Atmosphere   Normobaric Normoxic Atmosphere

Figure 2: Inert air compared to normal air at sea level and to air at mountain summit (illustration based on concept by Kotliar[26]).

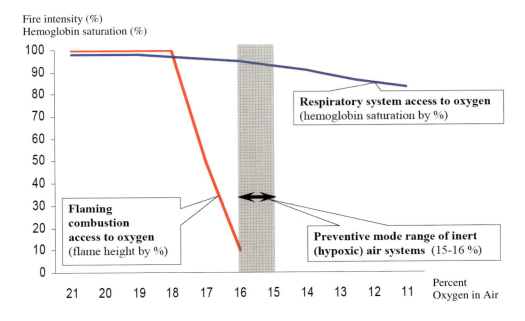

Figure 3: Effects of oxygen concentration in air for human occupation: On combustion (red curve) and on respiration (blue curve). Note range of typical inert air for fire prevention and limits for safe long term and short term occupation.

Combustion curve corresponds to stable flame height in experimental set ups. The affinity of O_2 to haemoglobin depends on its partial pressure only, while the kinetic of combustion depends on the proportion of O_2 in the gas mixture (ill. based on concept by Kotliar[26]).

In the wake of this discovery a number of research papers are being published. This report examines implications for protection of heritage.

Health Issues

Although human respiration is affected by hypoxic air no more than residing at elevations from sea level up to 2500 m altitude, there should be reason for concern if artificial atmospheres are established for normally occupied rooms near sea level. Several studies have been performed searching for side effects, and summarized in section 4.5. They consistently conclude favourably. The human body is able to perform well in 15-21 percent of oxygen in air, and some of the studies point out that most people get healthier from lowered oxygen levels.

The few individuals with predispositions that prevent them from living at high elevation or travel in aircraft cabins, should not occupy hypoxic air areas either.

1.2   Inerting Methods

Inert gases act to extinguish fires primarily by dilution of air. They do not take part in combustion processes and reduce the availability of oxygen to fuel fires. Carbon dioxide has been the most common in use. Nitrogen, argon and steam are also common, as are inert gas blends such as of nitrogen and argon. Helium and neon are possibilities, but less useful due to cost except for special applications such as magnesium fires.

The novel application of inert air, however, is the subject of this report. Inert air overcomes major drawbacks of conventional inerting methods, which will be apparent from evaluations made later, and in the case studies, of this report.

Methods of creating hypoxic atmosphere (inert air) in a room volume:

- Continuous inerting by controlling pure nitrogen feed into room
- Continuous inerting by premixed hypoxic air feed into room
- Inerting on demand (automatic systems containing premixed hypoxic air)

The continuous systems are usually preventative systems while "on demand" systems are suppression or extinguishing systems to fight established fires.

Different technologies and patented intellectual property rights have led to manufacturers of equipment following two routes; either nitrogen feeding or inert air feeding systems.

1.3   Application Potential for Museums and Historical Buildings

Hypoxic air inerting offers not only fire protection but also the potential benefit of a reduced oxygen atmosphere that may be more conducive to preservation of artefacts, building décor or fabric. Many characteristics of inert air offer promise and particular benefit in heritage applications.

The extensive benefits being put forward by the industry as set out below are analyzed as hypotheses in his report, with conclusions set out in Chapter 6.

- Prevents ignition (in contrast to gas extinguishing systems)

- Prevents smoke release prior to fire extinguishing (in contrast to gas extinguishing systems)

- Prevents backdraught (in contrast to gas extinguishing systems)

- Reduced degradation of artefacts and fabrics

- Fully benign to environment (in contrast to halon and many other gas extinguishing systems)

- Not toxic, no residue, no corrosive risk (in contrast to some other extinguishing media)

- Allows considerable room air leakage (in contrast to gas extinguishing systems)

- Allows open doors for rescue of artefacts, manual intervention, evacuation (in contrast to gas extinguishing systems)

- Do not have limited extinguishant reservoirs (in contrast to gas extinguishing systems)

- No refilling, transport or resetting issues following incidents

- Applicable to small vital rooms and vaults

- Applicable to very large room volumes (galleries or multi-storey, multi-room historic buildings)
- Applicable to moderately leaky historic rooms where fixed permanent seals are not acceptable
- Applicable to protection of artefacts which are extremely sensitive to smoke, particles, water, corrosive gas or mechanical impact
- The inherent simplicity of inert air venting promises high reliability.
- No installation of nozzles, pipes etc in protected room (when inert air generators are integrated into new or existing air conditioning systems)

There are however a number of challenges presented by inert air systems in heritage applications which must be considered:

- Health risks for certain individuals in normally occupied or public spaces.
- Some fuels in special spaces like laboratories may require suppression mode and evacuation.
- Secondary effects of continuous high concentration of nitrogen on fungus or other biological processes thriving by nitrogen.
- Nitrogen feed systems may give rise to uneven oxygen levels and require complex measures to ensure safe inerting, especially at multi-room facilities.
- Failure of venting system to safely dispose surplus oxygen from generators.
- Power consumption of equipment may give rise to high energy costs.
- Accommodating equipment where no mechanical ventilation systems suitable for use exist may present difficulties in historic buildings (as with conventional extinguishing systems), in terms of space, inert air ducting and noise.

The pros and cons of inert air in protecting heritage are the subjects of this report – and are examined in chapter 4 and 5 in particular.

1.4 Hypoxic Air versus Other Fire Protection Alternatives in Museums and Historical Buildings

A qualitative comparison of fire protection options in heritage environments is shown in figure 4. It is useful for a qualitative discussion of parameters and for overview, but is not intended to form the basis of decision making.

The figure shows a favourable ranking of inert air venting based on the lack of secondary damage risks, and on the simplicity, related to the concept.

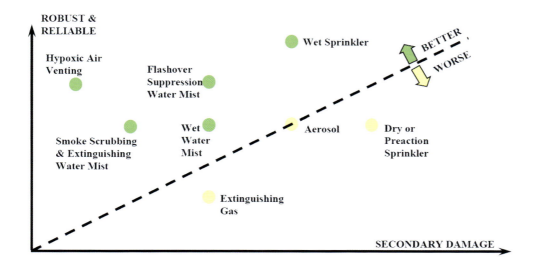

Figure 4: A qualitative comparison of two vital properties of fire protection systems for heritage.

CAUTION: The illustration does not apply to any single object, and is based on evaluation of risk of secondary damage and robustness/reliability. Thus, aesthetics, cost, maintenance, space requirements etc are NOT considered in this evaluation (see elsewhere in this report for evaluation of the latter properties).

2 HYPOXIC AIR SYSTEM CONCEPTS

There are two basic concepts for providing hypoxic air: Either continuously feeding nitrogen to protected rooms until the hypoxic air blend is attained, i.e. *nitrogen feed*, or to provide premixed hypoxic air, i.e. *hypoxic air venting*.

2.1 Nitrogen Feed (Continuous)

An hypoxic air atmosphere may be created by suppling nitrogen to a protected room so as to keep the oxygen level hypoxic. This is the first technique to make a breathable, yet inert, atmosphere. (See 2.2 for "hypoxic air venting" for supplying premixed hypoxic air, instead of measured nitrogen quantities, to rooms).

Oxygen content of room is controlled using patented conditioning technology[19]: The level of control is so precise as to allow occupation with no side effects while a fire cannot start. Such a system has been available since 2001, and 50 installations are reported to have been delivered by 2003 – varying from small IT rooms to warehouses of more than 100 000 m^3. A VdS (Verband der Sachversicherer, Germany) approval is reported to have been obtained in late 2003 (not confirmed). See Appendix B for details.

2.2 Hypoxic Air Venting (Continuous)

The principle of "hypoxic air venting" promises the most for heritage applications, and prompted this report. The term "inert air venting" is synonymous.

The principle contrasts feeding nitrogen and controlling the room atmosphere by sensors, regulating valves/vents and fans to circulate air at high ceilings - as required by nitrogen feed systems. Inert air venting has more benefits compared to conventional nitrogen feeding, in particular for heritage applications where installations in the protected rooms are not wanted and where a consistent and safe hypoxic air mixture is vital. The concept of hypoxic air venting is the subject of a number of patents [24-30]. See figure 4 for applications of the concept and appendix B for details. The concept offers benefits which are being adopted by the industry. It allow two different operational modes: preventive and extinguishing. An explanation of the modes explained, based on patent application texts, follows: [20, 24-30]:

Extinguishing mode
The agent is simply hypoxic (oxygen reduced) air. This is air containing 10-12% by volume (variable) O_2 and approximately 87-89% N_2 by volume.

Ignition Prevention Properties: At 15.2% O_2 by volume, *Class A* fires are extinguished*, and at 14.3% O_2 by volume, *Class B* fires are extinguished.[1] Interestingly, ignition prevention or inerting occurs at approximately 17% O_2 by volume. This information can be extrapolated from inerting values regarding IG-100 in National Fire Protection Association Standard 2001.

---

* Extinguishment O_2 figures are a the extreme conservative end of the test spectrum. Most figures point to O_2 extinguishment percentages between 15-17% O_2 by vol.

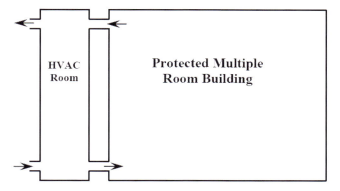

NO FIRE PROTECTION

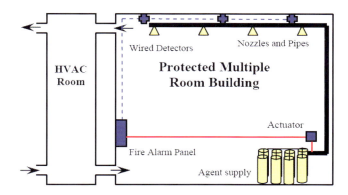

EXTINGUISHING SYSTEM
Conventional

FIRE PREVENTION AND EXTINGUISHING
Hypoxic Air Venting

Figure 5: The simplicity provided by inert (hypoxic) air systems (bottom) is illustrated by conceptually comparing conventional gas or water based extinguishing systems (middle). Architectural or aesthetically invasive installations are avoided with the inert air concept, which prevents rather than extinguishes fires (Illustration by COWI).

Preventing mode

A fire preventative normobaric hypoxic environment provides a revolutionary solution in fire protection. In preventative mode, the environment in a normally occupied facility is perpetually maintained at 15-16% oxygen which is healthy for human occupants (15-16% O_2 at sea level corresponds to an altitude of 2600-2100 meters in terms of O_2 partial pressure.) This preventative environment significantly reduces the possibility of the ignition of the majority of common flammable materials. This is further explained in section 4.5.1.

2.3   Inerting on Demand (Automatic Extinguishing)

Hypoxic air on demand resembles conventional extinguishing systems employing inert gases and hence is not extensively covered by this report.

Both nitrogen, and premixed hypoxic air, feed systems may operate on demand:

1   To act as automatic or manual extinguishing systems during public occupancy during exhibition hours

2   To provide superior extinguishing systems to conventional inert gas systems - where the installation of 24 hour inerting is not feasible due to large leakage rates or other provisional arrangements

Inerting on demand is not recommended if avoidable as it involves most of the drawbacks of conventional inert gas extinguishing, such as reliability issues from detection dependability, actuator dependability etc.

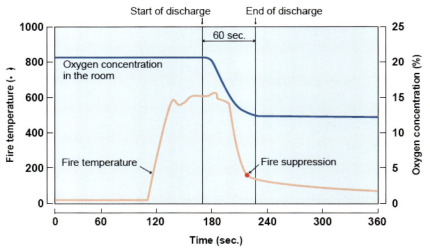

Figure 6: Extinguishing sequence with pure nitrogen system. For comparison only - note that oxygen concentrations with typical hypoxic air venting systems are 15-17% (Ill. by Koatsu Co[51]).

Such systems are like ordinary extingushing systems including detectors and actuating mechanisms, except they:

- Contain premixed hypoxic air
- Are refilled on site automatically
- Allow occupation for extended or limited period depending on concentration

Conventional inerting on demand, i.e. extinguishing system using inert gas(es), are out of scope of this report.

---

3   REGULATION, STANDARDS AND AVAILABILITY

3.1   Regulatory Bodies

Inert air venting is not yet covered by any known building regulation codes.

The United States Federal Aviation Administration has proposed retrofit of all commercial aircraft fuel tanks with hypoxic ventilation[20].

3.2   Standards, Approval Bodies, Installation Guidelines

No approval standard, listing body or independent installation guidelines for inert air venting yet exist. The insurance industry offers an exception, though, see below.

Given the relative simplicity, there is hardly a need for elaborate standards. The fire preventive and retarding performance at given percentages of oxygen, and allowed percentages of oxygen of inert air venting systems for various occupational rooms ought to be agreed upon by industry, and limits set by authorities.

Note: Inert air systems may not, by inherent design, dump dangerous concentrations of nitrogen or any other substance. Systems produce safe inert air and the fail-safe mode is pure air. If internal monitoring fails the systems are not capable of lowering oxygen levels more than slightly over a long period, which is readily detected by an outlet sensor.

Nitrogen feed systems, however, involve some complexity and hazards that would need to addressed by standards – but, currently, it appears nitrogen feed systems are less favoured.

3.2.1   Insurance

The new concepts of continuous inerting are too novel to be readily accepted by the insurance industry granting rebates. However in 2004, one large world-wide insurer, Allianz Risk Consultants, issued a "Loss Control Guideline"[10] titled:

- *"Requirements for Buildings with Permanent Inertisation Concepts"*

The document reports on experience with inerting installations in the previous 10 years. Problems have been noted with excessive leakage rates either caused by the building structure or by unforeseen frequent transport of goods through openings. Leaking also caused unplanned oxygen reduction in a neighbouring room in a case of freezer storage room of 30m height. Basically, excessive leakage seems to be the only drawback identified.

One should be aware that the considerations in that document relate to industry applications and large storage buildings/rooms. Furthermore, the document seems to be dealing with nitrogen feed concepts, although its scope does allow for "other concepts".

Insurance Rebate

The Allianz Loss Control Guidelines for the insurance industry state:

"Due to lack of experienced based knowledge: No rebates until further notice. For those occupancies where there is no other option a rebate comparable with gas extinguishing or partial sprinkler systems could be applied"

Considering the general conservative approach of the insurance industry, and the novelty of the current concepts, this statement is remarkably favourable.

3.3   Market Availability

Inert air systems are available in the market. Successful applications depend on choosing the optimum concept and implementing installations to work in unison with air conditioning, ventilation and heating utilities of buildings.

Judging from experience of the initial inert air installations, one should seek independent professional assistance in order to avoid pitfalls and keep energy consumption low.

Nitrogen Feeding

A number of companies manufacture membrane separators used by vendors of pure nitrogen feed systems, especially for ships where such systems have been successful over 20-30 years. These systems are large and cannot be classified as hypoxic air systems as oxygen content is below 8% and preventing protected cargo rooms from being occupied. The main objective is preservation of fruit etc.

One fire protection company applying such products for nitrogen room feeding to create a hypoxic, fire safe atmosphere for occupation reports of approximately 50 installations in Europe. See appendix B for known manufactured products.

Hypoxic Air Venting (inert air venting)

One company pioneered and holds the intellectual property rights for hypoxic air venting, i.e. generators feeding premixed and precise hypoxic air into rooms to be protected.

For Europe, a number of companies are expected to offer hypoxic air venting by license. At the time of writing the position is not yet settled.

4 IMPLICATIONS FOR HERITAGE

4.1 Potential Applications

For museums and historical buildings, inert air venting for fire protection and reduced degradation of artefacts and fabrics is feasible for any room category or complete buildings. See Table 3 for a listing of room categories.

The constraints are energy cost in some applications, and access control to prevent individuals with certain predispositions from entering protected areas, similar to boarding aircraft.

4.2 Fire Prevention

There is no doubt about the fire preventive and retarding performance of hypoxic air, but there is doubt about what are optimum concentrations of oxygen for various room categories and room contents.

If one accepts an oxygen starved fire producing some smoke over a period of time until manual intervention, concentrations may be set within health safety limits which require no access control, special permits or considerations.

There is a lack of research on fire prevention in hypoxic air, which is discussed elsewhere in this report. Work carried out by Berg and Lindgren (2004) acknowledges this, and their study is further commented on in appendix A.

We strongly recommend that the simple research required to fill the gap is carried out.

4.3 Reduced Degradation of Artefacts

This section discusses the effect of decreasing oxygen in the environments of artistic or historic works. It will be shown, for the material studied in the examples, that reducing the amount of oxygen around them will diminish deterioration.

One of the most quoted early investigation of a low oxygen environment for preservation purposes is the Russell and Abney Report of 1888 (Brommelle 1964) (Hansen 1998), "Action of Light on Water Colours".

Russell and Abney concluded that the presence of moisture and oxygen was necessary for a change to occur. Several colorants found in the watercolours they studied would fade less when exposed to light in vacuum. The findings prompted the design of an airtight container for oil paintings and watercolours, which was patented in 1893.

A very well known expert among conservators and curators is Garry Thomson. In "The Museum Environment" (Thomson 1986) he deals with the problem of air pollution and discusses the importance of reducing Sulphur dioxide and Nitrogen dioxide to not more than 10 $\mu g/m^3$ and Ozone to trace levels=0-2 $\mu g/m^3$.

Thomson points out that when a fuel is burnt the sulphur combines with oxygen in the air to form sulphur dioxide. Sulphur dioxide itself is only a mild acid. However it quite readily combines with further oxygen to form Sulphur trioxide, SO_3. As soon as this is formed it combines with water molecules to form sulphuric acid, a very strong and corrosive chemical.

The role of oxygen present is clear.

$$S \quad + \quad O_2 \quad = \quad SO_2$$
sulphur   oxygen   sulphur dioxide gas

$$2SO_2 \quad + \quad O_2 \quad = \quad 2SO_3$$
sulphur dioxide   more oxygen   sulphuric trioxide gas

$$SO_3 + \quad H_2O \quad = \quad H_2SO_4$$
sulphur trioxide   water   sulphuric acid

Oxygen of course also plays a role when different Nitrogen oxides are formed. Nitrogen dioxide is a worry for conservators and curators. Like sulphur dioxide it is soluble in water.

$$NO \quad + \quad \tfrac{1}{2}O2 \quad = \quad NO2$$
nitrogen oxide   oxygen   nitrogen dioxide

$$2NO_2 \quad + \quad H_2O \quad = \quad HNO_2 + HNO_3$$
nitrogen dioxide   water   nitric acids

Ozone, O_3, is a powerful oxidant, Thomson talks of a "destroyer" of almost all organic material. Ozone is created in two processes, one natural and one artificial. Natural ozone is formed in the upper atmosphere by UV radiation.

$$O_2 \quad = \quad O \quad + \quad O$$
oxygen   oxygen atoms oxygen atoms

$$O \quad + \quad O_2 \quad = \quad O_3$$
oxygen atoms more oxygen   Ozone

The artificial production of Ozone is mainly a photochemical process as a result of car exhaust gases and sunlight. Some electrical devices such as certain kinds of lamps and electrostatic air filters can generate Ozone. Mercury vapour lamps with quartz envelopes used in photocopiers generate Ozone.

If the substance that makes up a museum object or the interior decoration of a historic building reacts with oxygen, the resulting oxidative chemical processes can cause physical changes, such as brittleness and cracking, as well as chemical changes, such as colour fading.

Museum objects and interior decoration are normally complex combinations of different substances. There are many kinds of deterioration besides those caused by oxygen which make it difficult to predict what protection from deterioration would be given to a particular object, if it were placed in a hypoxic air environment or an inert-gas environment.

The chemistry of oxygen's reactions with several classes of materials such as celluloses (paper, linen, cotton, wood) or proteins (parchment, vellum, skin) or colorants is today well known[60].

In summary, it is clear that removal of oxygen will hinder development of brittleness and loss of fibre strength in non-acidic celluloses[60].

Proteins typically constitute parts of historic and art objects. Collagen is the principal protein of animal skins, and thus is the major constituent of parchment (from goats and sheep) and of vellum (from lambs, kids and calves). An oxygen-free environment would preserve pertinacious materials by reducing the oxygen related deterioration[60].

Colorants (dyes and pigments in watercolours) have been mentioned in this chapter as subjects of the earliest conservation studies using a reduced-oxygen environment. However some colorants are reported to fade more rapidly in the absence of oxygen than in its presence[56].

In 2003, the Swedish National Heritage Board published the results of an evaluation project concerning storage of museum objects in an anoxic environment. (Riksantikvarieämbetet, Stockholm, 2003, "Syrefria mikroklimat", ISBN 91-7209-321-89) Some of the project's research is of interest for this paper and abstracts follow:

Abstract from Conservator Katarina Lampel: ***"Long time storage of archaeological metals in hypoxic air".***

"Iron artefacts from archaeological sites are usually stored for a long time, before the conservation treatment can start. In most cases they are not treated at all. The relative humidity in the storing place is often too high and the artefacts corrode. Oxygen and humidity must be present for the corrosion process to start and be maintained. The ideal storing place for archaeological iron would be a dry, oxygen-free microclimate. In this test an oxygen-free microclimate was created, using an oxygen absorber and barrier film.

Sixty iron nails from different archaeological sites were enclosed in three different climates.

1.   Oxygen-free using bags of Escal® laminated plastic film combined with an oxygen absorber (Mitsubishi, RP-Agent 05A®).

2.   Dry but not oxygen-free, using bags of Escal® laminated plastic film together with Silica gel.

3.   As a reference, only in zip-bags of polyetene.

The artefacts were kept in the bags for three years, after being weighed and documented by photography and X-ray photography.

At the end of the testing period, the amount of oxygen in the dry enclosures was measured. The oxygen-free enclosures were completely airtight. The artefacts were documented once again in the same way as before. Neither the iron nails that were kept in the oxygen-free microclimate nor the nails in the dry climate showed any further corrosion. The weight was reduced by 1% in average, due to loss of moisture. The nails that were kept in the plastic bags were badly corroded and their weight increased by 7.4% in average, due to the corrosion products formed".

Abstract from Conservator Charlotte Ahlgren: *"Degradation of paper by iron gall ink corrosion in hypoxic air"*.

"It is acknowledged that the degradation of paper by iron gall ink corrosion is caused by acid hydrolysis in combination with oxidation of cellulose. The aim of this study was to determine whether an oxygen-free microclimate could retard the ink-corrosion process by affecting the rate of oxidation.

Samples were made up by applying iron-gall ink to handmade rag and newsprint papers. The papers were subsequently housed in individual encapsulations at different conditions: at 30 or 60% RH, with or without oxygen absorbers, for the duration of three years. An accelerated ageing test was also carried out.

The mechanical strength of the paper samples was evaluated by means of folding endurance tests (ISO 5626). On two samples the surface of the paper was analysed by means of Electron Spectroscopy for Chemical Analysis (ESCA).

The result of the mechanical testing did not show any significant difference in paper strength for the cotton based paper. However, for the newsprint paper the folding endurance was found to be enhanced after storage in oxygen free atmosphere, before and after accelerated ageing.

Future studies might focus on the side effects of an airtight storage enclosure. Volatile compounds which are released from ink or paper are trapped in the enclosure. The potentially harmful effects of these gases and whether they belong to the compounds which are removed by the oxygen absorber should be investigated.

Further research on the effects of oxygen free environment on material suffering from iron gall ink corrosion is necessary, before the method should be implemented as a preservation method".

Abstract by Conservator Kerstin Petersson: *"The influence of oxygen-free microclimate on cotton fabric dyed with natural Indigo"*.

"The research aimed to see if, and and how, the colour in textiles dyed with the vat dye Indigo (*Indigofera tinctoria*) was affected by long time storage in an oxygen free microclimate. Ageless® is often used as an oxygen scavenger during these treatments. Did Ageless® affect the indigo dyes?

Cotton test fabric was dyed with natural Indigo. Samples with undyed cotton were sewn towards the dyed sample to see if there should be a colour staining on adjacent fabric during the test. The samples were then prepared in different ways; in between acid free paper (usual for objects in museum storages); inside airtight plastic enclosures flushed with nitrogen gas before sealed and equipped with bags of Ageless® as extra oxygen scavenger; inside the same kind of plastic enclosures but with normal atmosphere. The prepared samples were then either put in museum storage (dark, 18-20°C, 45.50% RH) or in an eastern located window for three years.

The colours of the samples were measured according to Swedish standard SS 01 91 00 with spectrophotometer before and after the three year long test period. Visual measures against Greyscales were also made after three years to see colour changes (Greyscale colorchange 10-steps part number 39-9004-00) and also colour staining on adjacent fabrics (Greyscale staining 10-steps part number 39-9003-00).

No colour change could be detected in the Indigo dyed samples in the oxygen free environment, neither those put in the storage or in the window. Those put in between acid free paper in storage, and those in the window inside plastic with atmospheric oxygen inside the bag, had become lighter and had less colour tone".

Abstract from Conservator Jon Lönnve: ***"Consequences of oxygen free storage on inorganic pigments".***

"Long-term oxygen free storage of museum objects raises some aspects of consideration. One such aspect is colour change of different pigments. Question one: will inorganic pigments be affected by the exposure of an inert atmosphere? Question two: does oxygen in the surrounding atmosphere have an effect at all on pigments?

In this survey a number of different inorganic pigments were tested out in two different environments. One set of pigments was put in an oxygen free environment, while the other was placed in a high concentration environment of oxygen. Both samples were put in bags of oxygen barrier film and then stored in collection storage room. Oxygen scavengers were used in one of the bags. Analyses of the pigments were carried out by the use of the NCS colour analysing system before and after the storage. The exposure time was three years.

The result did not show any significant changes to the pigments. Under the circumstances of this test, oxygen free storage does not appear to affect the inorganic pigments tried out in this test. However, the test proved that light in combination with an inert atmosphere may change the appearance of some pigments".

Abstract from Conservator Jon Lönnve: ***"Storage of cellulose nitrate based material in oxygen-free environment".***

"Cellulose nitrate based material in museum collections is a potentially very destructive material. The polymer emits harmful corrosive nitrogen dioxide witch may attack surrounding artefacts. Cellulose nitrate also represents a significant fire hazard. The deterioration process of the material is autocatalytic and may result in auto-ignition. Humidity, oxygen and nitrogen oxides are three main deterioration factors that could be taken care of in modified atmospheres. In this project several test samples were packed in different enclosures, some in anoxia, and others with magnesium oxide and Zeolite. After four years the test samples were analysed with FT-IR as well as with a micro calorimeter.

The results indicate that anoxic storage of cellulose nitrate has a positive influence on the stability of the material".

Abstract from Conservators Monika Åkerlund and Jan-Erik Berg: *"Anoxic treatment of a larger natural history object".*

"The Veloxy® nitrogen generator system was tested for pest control in museums. In order to test the system on a big object a mounted bison cow was chosen. 20 larvae of *Attagenus woodroffei* was used as test insects. The item was enclosed in low diffusion film, consisting of nylon and polyethylene. The first test failed due to technical problems. In the second test the nitrogen level was reduced by an almost constant flow of humidity controlled nitrogen gas from the Veloxy®. The oxygen levels were measured through a canola under the skin of the item and in the outflow from the enclosure. The gas in the enclosure was exchanged three times and was then kept in a constant flow throw the enclosure.

After 61.5 hours treatment, the oxygen level in the surface of the object reached 0.22 % and the oxygen level in the outflow of the enclosure 0.4%. During the last eight days of the treatment the oxygen level under the skin of the item was below 0.1%. When the enclosure was opened at day 17, all test insects were dead. The control animals had a high survival".

Abstract from Jan-Erik Berg and Monika Åkerlund: **"Anoxic treatment for pest control of entomological collections".**

"Anoxic treatment was tested for pest control on plant and entomological collections. Veloxy® nitrogen generator and the oxygen scavenger Ageless® Z200 were used for reduction of the oxygen level. Cardboard boxes containing herbarium materials were tested, with larvae of *Trogoderma angustum* (Solier) and *Attagenus woodroffei* (Halsted & Green) as canaries. The oxygen level was reduced to 0.3% with nitrogen and 8 sachets of Ageless® Z200 were added. 100% mortality of both species was recorded after one week exposure.

Different kinds of wooden insect cases with glass lids (with one or two grooves) were tested with the same method. Test insects were larvae of *Anthrenus verbasci* (L) and *T. angustum*. Result with 2 sachets of Ageless® and two weeks exposure, both species survived. Result with 4 sachets of Ageless® and one week exposure, 21% survival of *T. angustum* in double-grooved cases. Result with 8 sachets of Ageless® and one week exposure, 100% mortality.

Based on this information a new test was designed where 4 sachets of Ageless® was added after reduction of oxygen level with nitrogen and survival was recorded after 4, 7, 10 and 14 days. Test insects were *A.verbasci, T. angustum, R. vespulae, Att. Woodroffei* and *Att. Smirnovi*.

LT 100: One grooved case, *A. verbasci, T. angustum, R. vespulae* and *Att. smirnovi* after 7 days. Double grooved case: *A. verbasci* and *Att.smirnovi* after 7 days. *T. angustum and R. vespulae* after 10 days, *Att. woodroffei* after 14 days".

All the tests carried out in the reported projects tried to identify the impact of low oxygen concentration in the environment on artefacts and historic buildings.

A literature search about the impact on artefacts in historic buildings under hypoxic environment yielded very little information. The Getty Conservation Institute has published "Oxygen-Free Museum Cases" (ed. Maekava 1998). The excellent "Conservation of Historic Buildings"[59] doesn't touch the subject. Neither does the

American Society of Heating, Refrigerating and Air-Conditioning Engineers[57] Handbook 2003, HVAC Applications, chapter 21: Museums, Libraries and Archives).

A professional search in the German, Italian and Russian languages may add some information to the subject, but the time-schedule for this report has been too narrow to allow such actions.

Summary on reduced degradation of artefacts

The literature studied and referred to in this chapter indicates clearly that an hypoxic air environment in a historic building or in a museum store or vault can positively contribute to the diminishing of normal deterioration of organic and non organic objects as well as interior decorations in historic buildings.

4.4 Reduced Degradation of Building Structure and Fabric

It follows from the results of section 4.3 that inert air does not add any substance or condition that are detrimental to building structures or fabrics.

It is clear that the reduced oxygen concentration is favourable in preserving common building materials as well as artefacts.

Still, 5% reduction of oxygen from 21 to 16% may not be compared to fully hermetic enclosures of near zero oxygen levels. We did not attempt to quantify preservation of continuous inert air on, for example, steel constructions which are corroded through time. Whether the expected reduced degradation versus oxygen concentration represents a linear correlation or not, we have not examined at this stage.

However, inert air for fire safety and preservation offer a definite benefit by not necessitating any non-reversible fixed installation or equipment invasion inside the protected structures. Thus, the building structures does not become subject to installation work, fixings, heavy pipes, maintenance work or accidental release of detrimental substances that are known drawbacks of conventional fire extinguishing systems. For implication of installations in detail, see section 4.8.

4.5 Health and Safety

4.5.1 Health effects on humans exposed to reduced oxygen concentration

This chapter discusses the effect of decreasing oxygen in occupied areas and the effects of occupation and working in permanent hypoxia.

Hypoxic means that partial pressure of oxygen is lower than normal, less than 21.2 kPa.

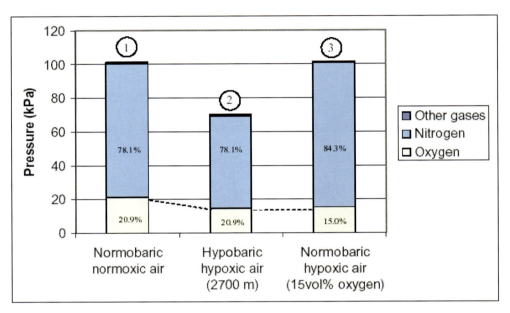

Figure 7: Comparison of normobar normoxic air, hypobaric hypoxic air and normobar hypoxic air.Column 1 illustrates natural sea level air condition to which majority of population is exposed. Column 2 illustrates natural air at altitude. Column 3 illustrates sea level air with oxygen level artificially reduced to that of altitude (Ilustration. by Linde et al (1994)

The only difference in normobaric hypoxic air and hypobaric hypoxic air is the total pressure. Many effects are comparable, because the oxygen partial pressure is the main factor that affects the body.

Hypoxia may be defined as "any state in which the oxygen in the lungs, blood and/or tissues is abnormally low compared with that of normal resting man breathing air at sea level"[66].

Environmental hypoxia is a common occurrence since a significant portion of the human population lives at high altitudes (>2500m). People can live at high altitudes because they adapt to the decreased atmospheric pressure.

Environmental hypoxia also occurs aboard submarines, because submarines are often kept oxygen deficient to decrease the risk of onboard fires. Chamber studies and experiments designed to replicate conditions found aboard submarines, have shown that exposures to normobaric hypoxic conditions might result in reduced cognitive performance. Gustafsson et al (1997) and Linde et al (1997) simulated normal work shifts on board Swedish and U.S submarines under normobaric hypoxic conditions. Linde et al. (1997) reported that effects on cognitive performance were found to be small and were prevented when the partial pressure of oxygen was maintained above 97.5 mmHg (97.5mmhg=13.67%O_2).

Exposure to environmental hypoxia under normobaric conditions can impair physical performance. Taylor and Bronks (1996) reported that in healthy young male subjects exercise times were reduced about 25% when performing moderate exercise (30 to 60 watt) on a cycle ergometer and breathing an oxygen- deficient atmosphere compared with exercise times recorded by the same subjects under normobaric conditions.

According to Baker and Hopkins (1998) training near sea level while living at an altitude of 2 500 m for a month enhances subsequent endurance performance, probably by increasing the oxygen-carrying capacity of the blood through an increase in production of red blood cells. A small proportion of athletes shows no improvement or even reduced performance with this "live-high train-low" strategy, but the enhancement for the average athlete is 2-3%. The extra red blood cells and the enhancement of performance are probably lost within 2-3 months after return from altitude[77].

In an effort to reduce the financial and logistical challenges of travelling to altitude training sites, scientists and manufactures have developed artificial altitude environments that simulate the hypoxic conditions of moderate altitude. In Finland they have build a "Nitrogen House" The nitrogen house is a standard-sized living structure that simulates the reduced oxygen level conditions of 2 500 m altitude by maintaining the air inside the house at higher levels of nitrogen and lower levels of oxygen in the house. Research conducted by Finnish sport physiologist Heikki Rusko on six elite cross-country skiers suggests that training in the nitrogen house is just as effective as training at altitude. Specifically, Dr. Rusko found that changes in critical blood markers, sub maximal heart rate, and sub maximal. Lactate was similar among athletes who trained in the nitrogen house compared to athletes who trained at an altitude camp[76].

Airline personnel and passengers are another group that routinely experience hypoxic conditions. Commercial jets operate under reduced atmospheric pressure, low humidity and mild hypoxic conditions. The Aviation Health Working Group (AHWG) has carried out studies of possible effects on health of aircraft cabin environment (2001). These show that inflight the air pressure in the cabin of a commercial aircraft is usually equivalent to that at 1 520-2 440 m, corresponding to between 17.4-15.5 volume % oxygen at sea level.

Oxygen Concentration	Symptoms
21%	None (normal oxygen level)
15%	No immediate effects
12%	Fatique, impaired judgement
10%	Dizziness, shortness of breath
7%	Stupor sets in
5%	Minimum amount that support life
2-3%	Death within 1 minute

Figure 8: Effects on human health associated with reduced oxygen concentrations (Ill. by Wagner)

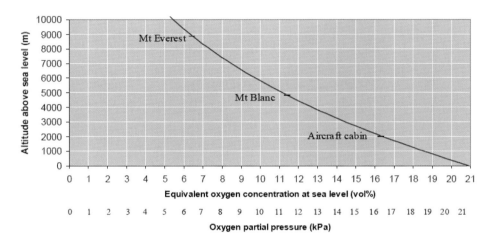

Figure 9: Equivalent oxygen concentrations at sea level and altitude (Ill. by Linde et al (1994))

The widely accepted minimum cabin pressure is equivalent to a maximum cabin altitude of 2 440 m. Based on evidence from research on the ground, it is plausible that some people will experience mild hypoxia at lower altitudes, the symptoms of which include impaired mental performance, reduced exercise capacity or fatigue. Some individuals suffer mild hyperventilation, headache, insomnia or digestive dysfunction. The effects are not great, and would not necessarily be of significance in most cases, although accident risk might increase. The risk would also depend on duration of the length of exposure to these conditions.

Oxygen reduced to between 15-13% in normobaric atmospheres is equivalent to the hypobaric atmospheres found at altitudes between 2 700 and 3 850 m. Acute mountain sickness occurs frequently at these oxygen partial pressures, but the full syndrome is rare if continuous exposure is limited to 6 hours. Persons suffering from cardiac, pulmonary, or hematologic diseases are however strongly recommended to seek medical advice before entering these altitudes.

4.5.2. **Occupational time in hypoxic atmospheres**

Working in hypoxia was studied by Angerer et al. (2003). Persons were exposed to 2 hours work within a reduced oxygen environment corresponding to 15 and 13 volume % oxygen at sea level. No effects were found on performance in cognitive and psychomotoric tests. No medical complication was found, but potentially endangered persons were excluded from the experiments.

Knight et al. (1990 a) exposed a test group to 13%, 17% and 21% oxygen atmosphere for 15 days (at rest and sub-maximal work rates designed to achieve 25% or 65% of the maximum rate of oxygen uptake). CO_2 levels were raised to mimic conditions on board submarines (from 0.03 %-0.9%). A significant reduction in arterial oxygen saturation (SaO_2) (83-85% under hypoxic conditions versus 94% at ambient conditions) was observed during exercise in atmospheres containing 13% and 17% oxygen. Despite decreases in SaO_2 , Knight et al (1990a) did not demonstrate a significant decrease in the volunteers' abilities to solve computational problems during exposures to moderate hypoxic conditions, even when subjects performed moderate exercise.

Mood and several cognitive and neurophysiologic functions are impaired when the oxygen concentration is less than 13 % volume in normobaric hypoxic air (Angerer et. al 2003).

Submariners live in an enclosed and isolated environment when at sea on submerged submarines. To protect submariners from potential adverse health effects associated with an oxygen deficient atmosphere, the National Research Council (NRC) of Canada convened a subcommittee on emergency and continuous exposure guidance levels for selected submarine contaminants in 2002. The calculated values of volume % of O_2 in Table 1 are based on a study carried out by this NRC subcommittee (NRC 2004).

Table 1 Emergency and Continuous Exposure Guidance Levels for Oxygen (mm Hg)

Exposure levels		Current US Navy Values		NRC Recommended
		Maximum	**Minimum**	**Minimum Values**
EEGL	1 h	220 (30.9 % O_2)	130 (18.2 % O_2)	105 (14.7 % O_2)
	24 h	160 (22.4 % O_2)	130 (18.2 % O_2)	127 (17.8 % O_2)
CEGL	90 day	160 (22.4 % O_2)	130 (18.2 % O_2)	140 (19.6 % O_2)

CEGL= continuous exposure guidance level. EEGL= emergency exposure guidance level.
NRC=National Research Council, Canada.

Occupation in hypoxia was also studied in the Biosphere 2 project (Walford). Four men and four women lived in a sealed environment for 2 years. During 13 months oxygen level declined to 14.2%, with minor effects on subjects only.

4.5.3 Recommendation on oxygen concentration in area categories

Type of occupation is the most crucial factor regarding the health aspect. Occupation can be divided into three categories: unoccupied, non public and public.

An unoccupied enclosure is a space where no humans are present at anytime. No considerations are required for health aspects and therefore any oxygen concentration could be chosen. Entering a hypoxic environment with less than 13% oxygen by volume will result in severe health effects. If the environment must be entered by humans the use of breathing equipment may need to be considered. The National Research Council (NRC) has recommended a minimum value for 1 hour occupation of 13.8% O_2 to protect submariners from potential adverse health effects associated with an oxygen deficient atmosphere.

A non public enclosure is a space where it is possible to control occupant access. The exposure time inside the enclosure must be controlled and preferably minimised. O_2 reduced to 15-13% in normobaric atmospheres is equivalent to the hypobaric atmospheres at 2 700-3 850 m altitudes. According to Angerer et al (2003) working in reduced oxygen environment corresponding to 15-13 volume % O_2 at sea level gives rise to no medical complication of healthy persons.

The most sensitive members of the population must be included when designing a hypoxic environment for public enclosures. Most of the occupants will cope in hypoxic conditions but the most sensitive people will suffer and may get severe symptoms.

NRC has recommended a minimum value for 24 hour occupation of 16.7% O_2. When you fly a commercial aircraft the air pressure in the cabin is usually equivalent to 1520-2440 m, which corresponds to between 17.4-15.5 volume % oxygen at sea level.

Some people are not allowed to fly commercial aircraft due to certain heart diseases or pregnancy. A similar ruling could be adopted for hypoxic environments.

In Table 3 typical room categories in museums are listed with recommended occupational times and respective oxygen percentages.

4.5.4 Impact on bacteria, virus, odours

Although no substantiating research is referred to, Red Brookes Laboratory/ Pyrogen[48] state that: "The unique properties of the hypoxic system will also provide mitigation for the stale or contaminated atmospheres in the airliner cabin. The system can remove bacteria, virus, odours and other nuisance products from the air conditioning system". Further investigations of these claims is required.

Table 2   Museum Room Categories

Room Category	Occupancy	Occupancy time per day (hours)	Minimum % of O_2 for acceptable hypoxic air – by health criteria
General public area	Public area	4	> 15.5 % (AHWG 2001)
Exhibition hall	Public area	4	> 15.5 % (AHWG 2001)
Laboratory	Staff area	8	> 15.5 % (AHWG 2001)
Examination room	Staff area	8	> 15.5 % (AHWG 2001)
Library	Public area	8	> 15.5 % (AHWG 2001)
Classroom	Public area	4	> 15.5 % (AHWG 2001)
Auditorium	Public area	4	> 15.5 % (AHWG 2001)
Counter	Public area	8	> 15.5 % (AHWG 2001)
Entry, vestibule	Public area	0.5 (8)	> 13 % (Angerer et al 2003) (> 15.5 % (AHWG 2001))
Corridor	Public area	0.5 (8)	> 13 % (Angerer et al 2003) (> 15.5 % (AHWG 2001))
Stairs	Public area	0.5 (8)	> 13 % (Angerer et al 2003) (> 15.5 % (AHWG 2001))
Toilet	Public area	0.5 (8)	> 13 % (Angerer et al 2003) (> 15.5 % (AHWG 2001))
Cloakroom	Public area	0.5 (8)	> 13 % (Angerer et al 2003) (> 15.5 % (AHWG 2001))
Shop	Public area	8	> 15.5 % (AHWG 2001)
Cafeteria	Public area	8	> 15.5 % (AHWG 2001)
Office - cell	Staff area	8	> 15.5 % (AHWG 2001)
Office landscape	Staff area	8	> 15.5 % (AHWG 2001)
Meeting room	Public area	4	> 15.5 % (AHWG 2001)
Lounge	Public area	8	> 15.5 % (AHWG 2001)
Elevator shaft	Public area	0.5 (8)	> 13 % (Angerer et al 2003) (> 15.5 % (AHWG 2001))
Storage room	Non public enclosures	1	> 13 % (Angerer et al 2003)
Magazine	Non public enclosures	1	> 13 % (Angerer et al 2003)
Laundry room	Non public enclosures	0.5	> 13 % (Angerer et al 2003)
Techn. control room	Non public enclosures	0.5	> 13 % (Angerer et al 2003)
HVAC room	Non public enclosures	0.5	> 13 % (Angerer et al 2003)
Display case/room	Unoccupied enclosures	-	> 13 % (Angerer et al 2003) (> 13.8)

4.5.5 Summary

Our literature survey has revealed fairly consistent recommendations for occupation at lowered oxygen levels. There is a gap between allowed limits for aircrafts and general (more strict) limits for enclosures at sea level. The rational of this discrepancy is open to question. If access to protected areas of buildings is controlled and persons with predispositions to relevant diseases are prevented from entering the area, exactly as for air flights, inert air of 15% O_2 should cause no concern. That means, inert air could be acceptable for all application categories of museums, libraries and historical buildings by simple precautions.

Additionally, because recommended limits of occupation until now have been based on systems that control feed of inert gas into rooms, known for uneven distributions, rather than premixed and safe hypoxic air feed, the limits ought to be reviewed since premixing technology introduces a substantial safety margin.

Table 4: Sample daily life environments posing accepted health risks

Health risks - public areas	Health risks - staff in fire protected premises

• Exposure to NO_x, SO_2, CO, CO_2 from:
  o Fossil fuel burning stoves
  o Traffic
• City centre dust pollution (PM_{10}, $PM_{2,5}$) from traffic
• Hypoxic air in aircrafts
• Populations at 1500-3000 m altitude
	• CO_2 gas extinguishing
	• Inert gas extinguishing
	• Fire dangers where there is no fire alarm or extinguishing systems
	
	(Staff risk inhaling smoke when fighting small fires, risk back draft from oxygen starved fires and may be trapped by accidental or real fire triggered CO_2 or inert gas releases)

A number of the everyday hazards faced by the general population is listed in Table 4, together with the possible hazards faced in a building fire situation. Taken in this context it could be argued that deployment of inert air with 13-17% oxygen content in protected spaces presents a lesser risk than these others listed - especially if people with medical conditions which make them predisposed to being affected are warned of the danger to them prior to entering. It is difficult to evaluate these different hazards by a single set of criteria and no comparative research exists demonstrating the relative risk posed by hypoxic air. Human populations living in naturally occurring high altitude conditions offer favourable pointers. Aircraft cabin conditions are however a better example to compare with hypoxic air building fire protection. In flight, passengers drawn from the wide population are subjected to sudden changes from normal to hypoxic air, and occupation times compare to those of rooms in buildings. Most likely, judging from experience from air flights - containing hypoxic air as used for inerting - hypoxic air venting is less of a risk than any of the other listed risks, when persons predisposed for being affected are warned - similar to boarding air flights. Experience from human population in areas high above sea level is also favourable, but air flights are a worst case to compare with hypoxic air venting because individuals are subjected to sudden changes from normal to hypoxic air, and the occupational times compare to those in rooms in buildings.

Finally, in complete contrast to the health concerns being considered, the references to athletic training in this chapter reveal that for the majority of the population, regular exposure and controlled exercise in inert air can improve health.

4.6   Secondary Damage

The possibility of secondary damage is considered in various sections of this report. As a summary, sections 1.3, 4.3 and 4.4 results offer clear evidence that inert air does not add any substance or condition that are detrimental to artefacts, building structures or fabric. Inert air for fire safety and preservation do not necessitate fixed or non-reversible invasive installations or equipment inside the protected structures, as will be explained in some detail in section 4.8.

Thus, the protected premises do not become subject of installation work, fixings, heavy pipes, maintenance work or accidental release of any detrimental substance. Such secondary damages or invasive actions effect on historic fabric and contents are known drawbacks of all other conventional fire extinguishing systems.

Preventing Backdraught
An argument put forward by some authors, including Berg and Lindgren[13], that inert air may incur or worsen the intensity of smouldering fires or increase the probability of backdraughts, supposedly in contrast to conventional gas extinguishing, is discussed in Appendix A. The findings of our research question the assumptions or rationale upon which this hypothesis is based. In fact, from present knowledge inert air will retard smouldering, prevent initiation of smouldering, reduce risk of backdraught and minimize the risk of personnel inhaling smoke from smouldering fires[9]. Indeed, in being preventative, inert air appears superior in this area to any other fire extinguishing methods. Exceptions may be water based systems cooling smouldering fires in solids, although only inert air will prevent and retard such fires if they are shielded.

4.7   Operating Modes

An hypoxic air venting installation may operate in any of two modes:

- Preventive mode: 15-16 % O_2 (staff occupy area occasionally or normally)
- Suppression mode: 10-12 % O_2 (short term occupation)

These are explained in section 1.2.

4.8 Installation

4.8.1 Inert air systems

The three basic designs are described in chapter 2:

1. Nitrogen Inerting (Continuous Regulated Nitrogen Feed)
2. Hypoxic Air Venting (Continuous Inert Air Venting)
3. Inerting on Demand (Extinguishing, or Suppression Mode)
   require different designs.

Continuous regulated nitrogen feed requires dedicated sensors in the rooms, a number of evenly spaced nitrogen inlets and an advanced control system to ensure sufficient and consistent oxygen concentration. This is challenging in high ceiling rooms, and fans for in-room circulation are recommended[13]. Local concentration variations still occur, and in general this system is best suited for unoccupied spaces. Due to these complexities it also tends to be more expensive.

Feeding premixed inert air into the space (hypoxic air venting) is by design most simple, least expensive and most safe, since the correct mixture of air can be guarenteed , at all times, throughout the space.

As explained in section 1.2 an hypoxic air venting installation may operate in any of two modes:

- Preventive mode: 15-16 % O_2 (staff occupy area occasionally or normally)
- Suppression mode: 10-12 % O_2 (short term occupation)

In suppression mode the installation act as a detector-activated extinguishing system, emptying a pressurized booster tank with a lower oxygen concentration and partly independent of emergency power. Evacuation is devised, although rescue personnel or other healthy individuals may occupy the protected area.

Alternatively, suppression mode activation can be done as a last resort to fight fires in special substances or conditions, although these will be rather unique.

Inert air installations does not require pipes, nozzles or other equipment in the room volumes to be protected, except for air inlets which often are combined with the ones for HVAC installation. Air inlets do not need to be evenly spread.

Compared to gas or water based extinguishing systems inert air installations are much less obtrusive (practically non-existent) in the rooms to be protected, whereas the hypoxic air generator and occasional pressurized booster tank may occupy as much space in plant rooms.

The size of generators depend very much of the normal leakage rate of rooms to be protected, and less on the total volume.

Inerting on demand, that is, if fire occurs, requires automatic fire detection and evacuation measures and procedures, which add cost and complexity. Inerting on demand is feasible with both nitrogen feed and hypoxic air venting systems.

4.8.2 Manufactured products

An overview of concepts and products as marketed is provided by Appendix B.

4.8.3 Design of inert air venting systems

The most simple and inexpensive way of establishing inert air protection for a museum store room is to locate an off-the-shelf stand alone unit inert air plant into the store room itself. This is the obvious reversible solution for single, unmanned rooms. The units are smaller than comparable gas extinguishing plants. However their in-built compressors may emit noise and heat which makes this solution less practical for manned spaces.

Where existing or planned air conditioning installations are available, one fortunate property of continuous inert air systems is that it can potentially be simply integrated into the air conditioning plant for manned and unmanned spaces requiring protection.

Where it is necessary to control the indoor climate and to compensate for leakage and emitted ions from materials and persons, HVAC plants will be in place. An HVAC plant circulates a large volume of air to be able to control the climate. Part of the air volume must be fresh air. The amount of required fresh air is a determining factor in selecting the capacity of the nitrogen generator.

A typical generator for this application will increase the demand for electrical energy of the complete HVAC system. In most applications, however, one can recover the heat produced by the inert air generator and use it in the building's HVAC systems. Therefore, the net increase of energy consumption can be reduced. To ensure control of the indoor climate and oxygen level at all times emergency power for the complete system is recommended.

Manufacturers report that the imminent introduction of next generation membrane separators for production of inert air is expected to be substantially more energy efficient, thus making inert air an even more practical proposition. This is also stated by the world-wide insurance company Allianz[52].

A typical proprietary system to connect into air conditioning plant consists of the required number of hypoxic generators, HEPA filters and oxygen monitor. A/c unit, smoke detectors and other supporting equipment are supplied with it.

Work is also under way to design integrated HVAC and inert air installations for the benefit of fire safety, preservation, energy consumption, reliability, cost, operational life time and maintenance (COWI).

Manual intervention applying water from hoses frequently causes unacceptable damage when fire has spread into roofs or attics. For inert air to provide an effective protection system for these areas, however, the local air exchange rate (ACH) must comply with design presumptions. A Nordtest method [44,45] takes into account local mean age of air in determining ACH, see Holmberg, J, "Protection of Attics and Roofs"[55].

For very high value applications consideration might be given to installing robust water mist back up systems in conjunction with inert air protection. It is likely 90-

99 % of 'fire' incidents will be prevented without any water release, while the risk of secondary damage from unintentional activations is substantially reduced.

4.8.4 Designs for minimum invasive installations

For protection of buildings or *multiple*-room facilities inert air systems may be incorporated in the building air conditioning plant, so that new installations are not required in the protected rooms. See figure 10 for an illustration of principle.

Ideally, in terms of pure fire protection performance, fully closed loop hypoxic air systems and ductless split AC systems are preferred. But variations exist, and some that provide minimum invasion in protected single rooms are shown below. See figure 10 for configurations for minimum invasion in multiple rooms.

For protection of *single* rooms only a number of options are available (some of these may not be preferred low-cost options for non-heritage applications):

1   Where dedicated ventilation exists, a generator may be incorporated into the supply duct.

2   Autonomous mobile unit in room. Connects to electric power outlet. Room ventilation and heat recovery remains unchanged. Fully reversible installation. The compressor may be remotely located to address the heat or noise problems it might pose.

3   Alternatively, the entire inert air generator installed remote from room with ducted connection to room (no ducts running in the room itself).

4   If the room is naturally vented by gap leakage only and one cannot accept new penetrations for grilles - and option 2 is not viable - neighbouring room(s), or intermediate sealed voids, may be slightly pressurized by inert air which then feeds into protected room via existing gaps. Alternatively, small bore penetration for pressurized inert air, or adapters that allow existing gaps to transfer pressurized air may be used.

Figure 10's illustrations are indicative only and do not show details required for *installation design* like outlets for oxygen and other byproducts at the generator units themselves. Note however, how the protected and sensitive areas become virtually free of invasive measures by these arrangements. Generally, existing air conditioning systems remain unaltered. Natural ventilation or ventilation by windows may be subject to restrictions in order to minimise inert air venting energy cost.

1 INCORPORATED IN HVAC ROOM, SUPPLY DUCT

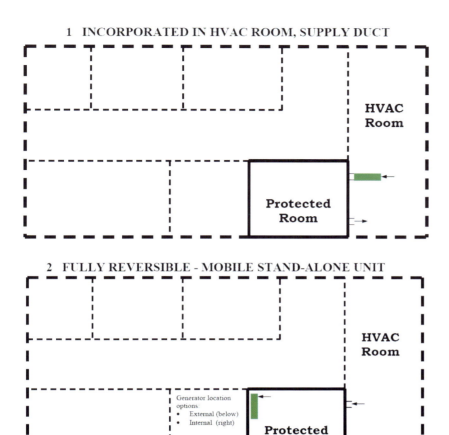

2 FULLY REVERSIBLE - MOBILE STAND-ALONE UNIT

3 MIGRATION BY LEAKAGE: MOBILE UNIT IN ADJOINING ROOM

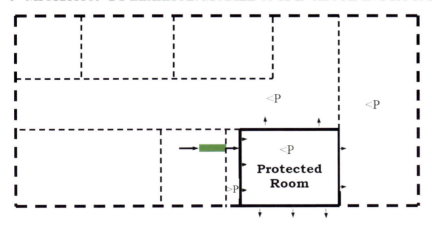

*Figure 10: Various means of hypoxic air inerting to avoid invasive installation in sensitive spaces.
See also figure 5.*

4.9   Maintenance. Energy. Lifetime Cost.

From the considerations reviewed in section 4.8, inert air venting seems destined to become the least expensive system that requires the least maintenance and yields best life time cost among available fire protection systems.

Guide costings gleaned from manufacturers suggest that at the time of writing hypoxic air generators for a 150 m^3 room may cost EUR 20 000 depending on airtightness and requirements. A room of 100 m^3, if leakage minimised, may cost EUR 8 000. The latter involves one 500 W unit weighing 23 kg.

In this report, allowance for the necessary adjustments to integrate inert air systems with building ventilation and/or air conditioning systems, and the energy consumption in particular, from running the generators (compressors) full-time, have been calculated roughly. Insufficient data from real installations has yet been gathered to conclude on cost. License agreements may also increase the cost of inert air venting systems.

Once the stage is reached where tenders for typical heritage applications are obtained for a number of projects, firmer costs for investment, maintenance and operation should become evident.

4.10 Challenges in Need of Research

Inert air venting can be applied based on current knowledge.

For applications in public areas, and to ensure optimum energy consumption and life time costs, however, we recommend further exploration of these areas prior to proceeding:

- Energy efficiency measures to optimize energy cost
- A review of required air exchange rates in inert air spaces
- Inhibition effect on smouldering combustion
- Fire heat and smoke retarding effects and damage per minute in hypoxic air.
- Oxygen concentration limits for prolonged personnel occupation in inert air
- Reliability of hypoxic air generators (a. operational, b. mixing consistency).

The above topics are discussed in relevant chapters of this report. The topics are not specific to any category of building, but stakeholders of museums and historical buildings - a potential major market for inert air venting systems - should consider clearing these challenges to inform adoption of the technology.

5 CASE STUDIES

5.1 **Introduction**

Inert air system designs must take into consideration several factors such as:

- Functional and physical compartmentation of the building areas
- Ventilation conditions (system configuration, infiltration conditions)
- Occupancy type
- Occupancy time per day
- Type of artefacts stored
- Type of building structure
- Protection, conservation and presentation requirements
- Risk of fire

The suggested acceptable hypoxic environments, based on health consequences, which are used in this chapter, are based on the previous discussions and conclusions in chapter 4.5 Health and Safety.

For all areas in general, and especially visitor areas, it might be a good solution - where practical - to apply higher oxygen concentrations during opening hours. This would enable health concerns to be overcome whilst still reducing the possibility of fire.

Dependant of ion emissions from building materials, infiltration by outdoor air and local building code limits, the fresh air demand varies from case to case.

The power estimates made for each case are based on two different requirements: 1 exchange of air per day and 12 exchanges of air per day, respectively. This makes a broad range of energy demand. Our energy estimates of the case studies are based on an estimated power of 0.1 kW per m^3 hypoxic air supply. In most cases the energy consumed by compressor units of hypoxic air installations can be recycled in the air-conditioning units.

Due to both the technical constraints of the hypoxic air and inert air system and the previously discussed consequence of hypoxic air and inert air on building structures and installations, as well as humans and artefacts, it seem most reasonable to divide the system into several sub-systems or single systems serving different areas of the building.

Considerations for minimum invasive installation
In the case studies, the most straightforward installations are considered. However, if by scrutiny on site obstacles arise, the various options listed in section 4.8.4 could be considered.

5.2   **Arezzo Public Library** (Italy)

Client: *Mr Luca Nassi*, Ministry of Interior. Fire Department of Siena.
Information: *Stefano Marsella.*

Pretorio Palace is one of the most famous buildings in the historic centre of the city. It is an example of Mediaeval and Renaissance architecture and derives from the union of three buildings built in 1200, belonging to the Guelph families of Albergotti, Lodemari and Sassoli. In 1209 Palace Albergotti became the seat of the Captain of Justice and in 1404 Palace Sassoli, purchased by the city-state, was turned into a prison. In 1632 Palace Albergotti was also purchased by the Municipality and the prison was enlarged. In 1926 the prison was moved to another building in Garibaldi Avenue and restoration works then started under the supervision of Architect Giuseppe Castellucci. Such works allowed the Mediaeval Museum and the Municipal Gallery to be hosted in the Palace. The palace shows inside the signs of ancient occupancies and arbitrary restoration operations, with a pragmatic use of architectural and sculptural elements as ornaments and furnishings. A coffered ceiling dating back to the 1600s was removed from the city monastery in 1930 and placed into the Library Director's office. On the mezzanine one can admire a gothic stone tabernacle containing a fresco of the Spinelli school and decorated with the typical cornice of arches and lobate endings. All rooms of the Palace witness the different historical periods with frescoes, wooden ceilings and sculptures, which lead visitors' imagination to the past.

Figure11: Arezzo Public Library

As shown in figures 12-15, the building holds archives and study rooms as well as conference rooms and general service rooms.

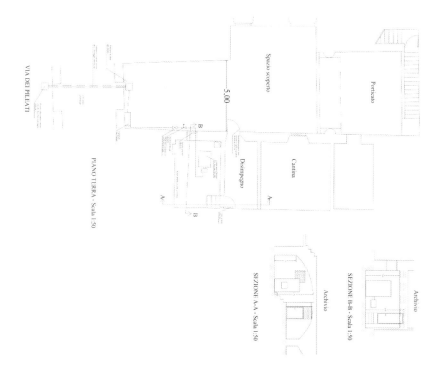

Figure 12: Basement

Figure 13: Ground floor

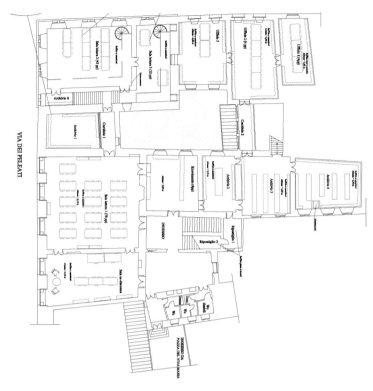

Figure 14: Mezzanine floor

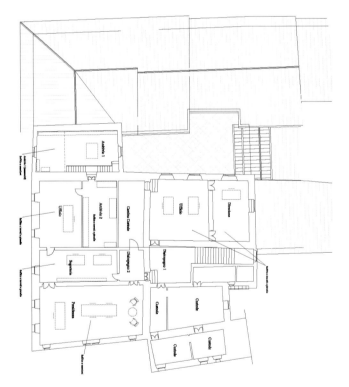

Figure 15: Second floor

The collection at Arezzo Public Library contains 145,000 items, among which there are books, and documents dating from the 13th century. Moreover, there are window glasses, frescoes and marble decorations, which are valuable items in terms of susceptibility to become damaged by, smoke, heat, corrosive gases, water, mechanical impact etc. During daytime from 8:30 – 17:00 the building is occupied by staff and visitors.

Today the building is naturally ventilated only and there is about 0.2 cm openings around windows and doors. About 50% maximum, of the opening area of door(s) may realistically be open at a fire incident.

The building is constructed of brick. It has no voids, shafts etc currently holding or being used as ducts, or such that may be used as air ducts. It is difficult to find available space for inerting system equipment or indeed space to dedicate to extinguishing systems only.

In addition to general concerns about applying conventional automatic extinguishing systems (water based, gas etc), this building offers the following challenges:

- water based: difficult to incorporate pipes or water reservoir
- gas: impossible to reduce building or single room leakages sufficiently to ensure gas holding time

In table 5 each area is described by occupancy type and period. The suggested hypoxic oxygen content of air and technical solution are shown in table 6.

Table 5 Building areas

Area	Occupancy type	Occupancy time in hours per day
Public rooms e.g. conference rooms, exhibition areas and general public area	Public	8
Study rooms	Public	8
Offices	Non-public	8
Technical/service rooms (e.g. toilets)	Non-public	0,5
Storage rooms	Non-public	0,5
Archives	Non-public	1

Figure 16: Heating plant and part of interior.

Table 6 Recommended hypoxic air solution

Area	Acceptable hypoxic air (health)	Recommended hypoxic environment	Technical solution
Public rooms e.g. conference rooms, exhibition areas and general public area	15.5-17.4 %	16 %*	Linked to compressor system/ Single, separate hypoxic air system / supported by natural air flow
Study rooms	15.5-17.4 %	16 %*	Linked to compressor system/ Single, separate hypoxic air system / supported by natural air flow
Offices	15.5-17.4 %	16 %*	Linked to compressor system/ Single, separate hypoxic air system / supported by natural air flow
Technical and service rooms (e.g. toilets)	13-15 %	15 %*	Linked to compressor system/ Single, separate hypoxic air system / supported by natural air flow
Storage rooms	13-15 %	15 %*	Linked to compressor system/ Single, separate hypoxic air system / supported by natural air flow
Archives	15.5-17.4 %	16 %*	Linked to compressor system/ Single, separate hypoxic air system / supported by natural air flow

* To be reviewed in detailed design

For this building, either of three different solutions might be feasible:

- Central hypoxic air unit; hypoxic air distribution by natural ventilation
- Local installations for selected areas
- Local hypoxic air units supported by one central compressor unit

If the natural air flow enables a stable and secure hypoxic air situation at the different areas of the building, supported from a central hypoxic air unit, this will be the most feasible solution, as in this case the installation makes no non-reversible changes to the building. However, such a solution has to be studied more in depth based on both air flow measurements and analysis.

Another solution might be to protect selected key areas, such as the archives, by local installations as shown in figure 17. This will protect the areas quite well, but the rest of the building will still be at risk. Adapting this solution, one also has to take into consideration the air leakage of rooms due to open doors and infiltration.

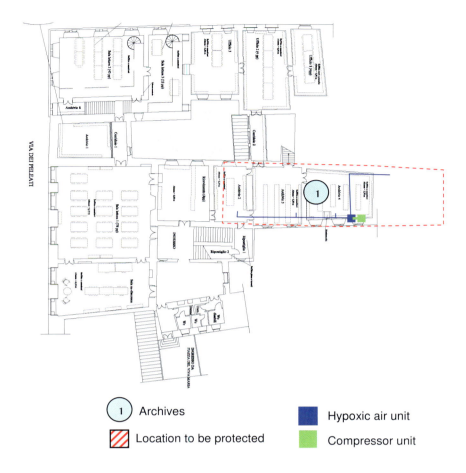

| 1 | Archives | | Hypoxic air unit |
| | Location to be protected | | Compressor unit |

Figure 17: Limited area installation

The last option is to install local hypoxic air units at several locations supported by a single central compressor unit. This makes a safe and controlled solution, but requires installation of both a relatively large hypoxic air unit and a piping system to distribute the compressed air.

For this building we estimate that the gross volume of the protected areas will be approximately 6000 m^3. With 1 air exchange per day this makes a power-demand of 25 kW, or 300 kW with 12 air exchanges per day.

5.3   Historic Scotland Stenhouse Conservation Centre

Client: Historic Scotland
Information: *Stewart Kidd*, Loss Prevention Consultancy Ltd

The subject being considered for protection is primarily used for the storage of archives and files relating to the work carried out by the Historic Scotland's Conservation Centre. The documents as such have no intrinsic financial or cultural value but their loss would inevitably impact on the work of the Centre, on the reputation of Historic Scotland and in a requirement to undertake additional work to replace the data destroyed. The most important impact of a wide scale loss would inevitably be the ability of a conservation specialist to be able to assess any deterioration in the condition of a property or artefact against previous surveys or work undertaken.

Figure 18: Historic Scotland: Stenhouse Conservation Centre

Description of Rooms to be Protected
The archive file storage room occupies the top floor of a three storey wing. The ceiling of the archive room is a barrel vault formed of tongue and groove jointed timber boards fixed directly to the timber roof structure above. The floor is of timber boarding on timber joists which are exposed as the ceiling finish in the library below. Preliminary inspection suggests that this floor construction would provide minimal fire separation between these two spaces. The floor of the library bears onto a masonry vault which is assumed to provide good fire separation from the ground floor electrical switch room below. Due to the assumed lack of effective fire separation between the library and file storage room it is considered that these rooms would require to be treated as a single space, with both provided with protection measures in order to safeguard archives on the top floor against fire.

Both rooms have three external walls constructed of sandstone onto which the plaster finish is directly applied. The remaining plastered internal stone wall of each room abuts a spiral staircase. Each room has a number of small windows and a door leading directly onto the spiral stair. These doors and frames are recent and comprise modern 30 minute fire resisting door sets whose junction with the wall masonry is sealed. The upper three sides of the frames are fitted with intumescent seals but there is no seal at the door thresholds. Doors are fitted with self closers, and 'fire door – keep shut' signage so are likely to be closed at all times except when being used to enter or leave the rooms. There is a fireplace in each of the rooms but these have been closed off with metal sheeting. It would be necessary for these to be checked for air tightness and possibly sealed at the edges.

Archive Storage Contents
Archives are housed in the archive file storage room within five purpose-built steel storage cabinets rated at two hours fire resistance. In addition there are presently a number of file storage boxes placed on top of the cabinets. It is not considered that the contents of this room are particularly at risk from either insect attack or growth of fungus.

The file storage room also contains a computer terminal, server and associated uninterruptible power supply.

Impact of Fire and Fire Fighting Agents
Any fire, heat, smoke or fire fighting activity using water would have a significant impact on the archives which are essentially paper based.

In a risk assessment of these premises carried out in 2003, it was suggested that the location would lend itself to protection by an inert gas fire suppression system. A budgetary price of €12, 000 was estimated for this. Consideration was given to the benefits of a water mist system but this was deemed inappropriate given the space needed for the storage of propellant gas and water, and possible issues of floor loading. While a water mist system was considered to be the least likely water based system to create excessive water damage post-fire, an inert gas system was considered to be the most appropriate when all factors were considered.

It is not considered that the contents of either room are at any risk from hypoxic air.

Occupation of Areas
The file storage room is generally unoccupied. Although a computer terminal is located within the space, as far as it can be determined it is visited by one or two people each day for no more than five minutes in connection with the use of the server. Once or twice each month, the room might be visited for longer if any detailed file searching needs to be undertaken. Greater use is made of the library which also has a computer terminal installed. Although this room is used for occasional study, no staff are actually based here, and all have desk space elsewhere in the building.

First floor

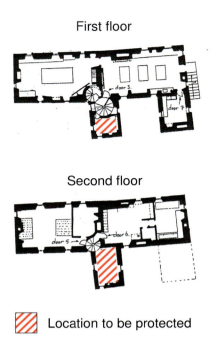

Second floor

Location to be protected

Figure 19: Location to be protected

Ventilation & Leakage Rate of Rooms to be Protected

The rooms are ventilated entirely naturally. The three windows in the file storage room and two windows in the library each have fixed glazing in their upper parts and their lower parts are fitted with solid wooden shutters which are hinged. It was not possible to determine the exact rate of air leakage / air movement. The window construction is not airtight and a relatively low temperature was noted in the rooms. Although no significant draughts were noted during inspection the situation may be different in high wind conditions.

Location of Inerting Equipment

Subject to consideration of impact on historic fabric, a possible location for the necessary hypoxic air equipment is within the protected top floor archive file storage room and/or the protected library below, with the compressor remotely located in the ground floor switch room – as shown in figure 20. Alternative configurations and locations in other adjacent spaces might also be considered during detailed design of a specific system installation for these premises.

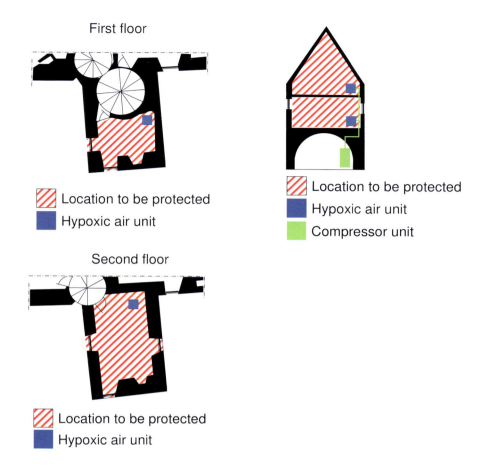

First floor

[ ] Location to be protected
[ ] Hypoxic air unit

[ ] Location to be protected
[ ] Hypoxic air unit
[ ] Compressor unit

Second floor

[ ] Location to be protected
[ ] Hypoxic air unit

Figure 20: Possible location of the hypoxic air system at Historic Scotland Stenhouse
Conservation Centre

Summary

Although the rooms to be protected are generally unoccupied, protection by a hypoxic air system providing a concentration of 16% O_2 (as deemed feasible for office space) would allow flexibility of access - as might be required on a day to day basis. The hypoxic air system here will require a single new self contained installation since the rooms to be protected currently solely depend upon natural ventilation. The air volume to be delivered might be relatively high per cubic metre due to the infiltration and air leakage inherent in the traditional construction. However, as the volume is small, relatively compact units of plant could meet the likely demand.

For this building we estimate that the total volume of protected areas will be approximately 97.5m^3. Assuming one air change per day, this makes for a power demand of 0.5kW; or up to 4.9kW if 12 air changes per day require to be allowed for. These figures represent gross energy consumption. However, when designing the installation, careful consideration should be given to the possibilities for energy recycling.

In this case the estimated theoretical minimum hypoxic air volume and energy demand should be considered indicative only and will be determined by actual infiltration in such an old building.

5.4   **Linnékuben** (Sweden)

Client: *Architect Myr Ullhammar.*
Information: *Professor, PhD Arne A. Anderberg.* Head of Phanerogamic
                    Botany and Palynological Laboratory Swedish Museum of
                    Natural History

Linnékuben and Botanhuset is a part of Swedish Museum of Natural History, Stockholm. The site was originally designed in 1907-1916 and the first collections were installed in the building as early as in 1915.

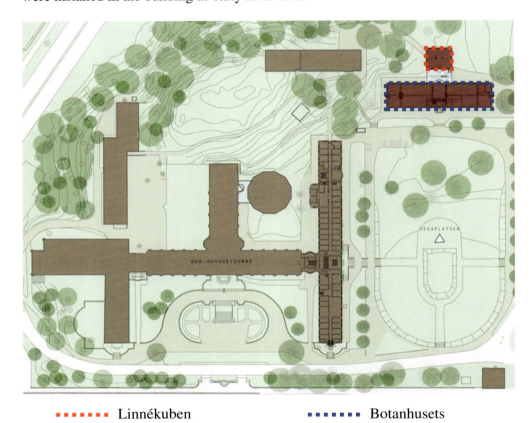

■■■■■■■ Linnékuben   ■■■■■■■ Botanhusets

Figure 21: Swedish Museum of Natural History with Linnékuben and Botanhuset

The Museum's collections include 22 million of specimens, and their size and quality places the Museum among the best in the world. The collections provide the basis for the research carried out in the scientific departments, and, through loans and visits by guest researchers, are constantly used by scientists and institutions throughout the world. It is a crucial role of the Museum to keep these collections available for international research, and to preserve them for future generations. The value of the collections is several tens of million euros.

The Linnean herbarium at the Swedish Museum of Natural History in Stockholm comprises some 4000 herbarium specimens, several of which are types formally designated by various experts. The specimens were once distributed by Linnaeus to his disciples and eventually they became part of the collections of the Royal Swedish Academy of Sciences, subsequently the Swedish Museum of Natural History.

Several studies have been carried out to evaluate possible expansion and redesign of Botanhouse, which is a part of Sweden's architectural heritage. The conclusion from this work so far, has been that it will be a better to construct a new building, called the Linnékuben, linked to the Botanhouse as shown figure 22.

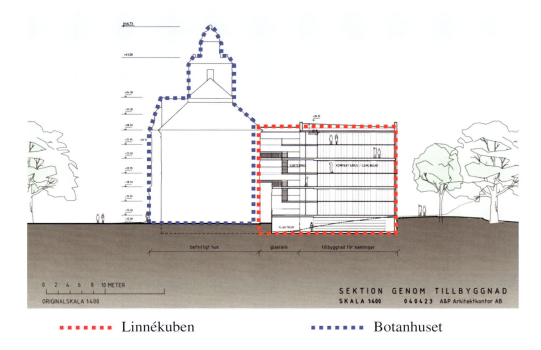

■■■■■■ Linnékuben   ■■■■■■ Botanhuset

Figure 22: Linnékuben and Botanhuset

The design draft of Linnékuben shows a modern building both with regards to building structure and details, as well as technical installations as ventilation and humidity control systems. The footprint measures 300 square metres with a gross area of 1725 square metres.

The primary purpose of this new building is storage of botanic plant material. The collections will be used in the ongoing research, and several scientists might visit the collection each year.

The herbarium samples are very sensitive to water and chemicals, as well as physical impacts. Chemical pollution might deteriorate the DNA. For many of these samples the DNA have not yet been investigated and documented.

The samples are vulnerable and exposed to insects such as Trogodema and Anthrenus vars larvas. Water exposure will increase the risk of fungus attack.

So far the effects of oxygen on these samples are not known.

In table 7 the different areas are described with occupancy type and time in hours per day. The suggested hypoxic environment oxygen content and technical solution are shown in table 8.

Table 7 Building areas

Area	Occupancy type	Occupancy time in hours per day
Offices	Non-public	8
Preparation rooms	Non-public	8
Technical and service rooms (e.g. toilets)	Non-public	0.5
Storage rooms	Non-public	0.5
Storage magazines	Non-public	1

Table 8 Recommended hypoxic air solution

Area	Acceptable hypoxic air (health)	Recommended hypoxic environment	Technical solution
Offices	15.5-17.4 %	16 %*	Linked to ventilation system/ Single, separate hypoxic air system
Preparation rooms	15.5-17.4 %	16 %*	Linked to ventilation system/ Separate hypoxic air system
Technical and service rooms (e.g. toilets)	13-15 %	15 %*	Linked to ventilation system/ Separate hypoxic air system
Storage rooms	13-15 %	15 %*	Linked to ventilation system/ Separate hypoxic air system
Storage magazines	15.5-17.4 %	16 %*	Linked to ventilation system/ Separate hypoxic air system

* To be defined in detailed design

As this building is not constructed yet, it gives a potential for implantation of a safe and efficient hypoxic air system. One of the challenges with the application of such a system is the installation and energy costs. However, in this building this can be taken into consideration when designing the ventilation, heating and fire fighting system. This gives a potential of efficient connections of the hypoxic air system to the ventilation system and energy recycling. With this, the proposed solution as described in table 8 will reduce both the probability of fire and the consequences of any fire in the whole building. Taking the acceptable hypoxic environment into consideration, this should not give any health impact to employees or visitors. It will also reduce the degradation of the building structures and the collections, as well as the risk of impacts due to technical errors on water-based fire fighting systems.

The hypoxic air venting design to this building depends on:

- Physical compartmentation of the areas
- HVAC system
- Type of occupancy

By description it appears that most of the building will be used for storage of botanic samples. The simplest design should therefore be to support the whole building from one system as shown in figure 23.

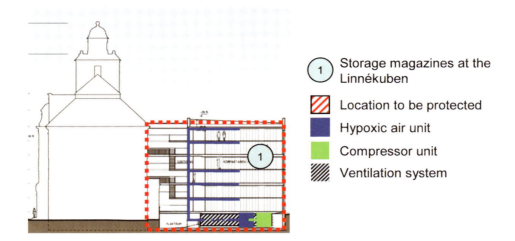

Figure 23: Suggested location of the hypoxic air system at Linnékuben

The volume of this building is estimated to 5200 m^3. At 1 air exchange per day the energy-demand is 21.7 kW, and is 260 kW with 12 air exchanges per day. This is gross energy-consumption. However, when designing the installations one should carefully consider the possibilities of energy recycling.

As the occupancy time in this building in general is very low one may expect a relatively low exchange of air per day, which reduces energy consumption.

5.5   Trøndelag Folk Museum (Norway)

Client: *Division Manager, curator Anne Sommer-Larsen.*
Information: *Curator Sander Solnes*

Trøndelag Folk Museum is one of the largest cultural history museums in Norway. It shows the building traditions in Trøndelag, from town and country, from mountain to coast and from Sami huts to city mansions.

The collection consist of the vintage buildings, artefacts and archives of the open air museum at Sverresborg, Trondhjems Sjøfartsmuseum (the maritime museum) and Meldal open air museum. Totally the museum's collections consist of more than 60 vintage buildings and more than 100 000 artefacts and historical photos.

The study objects at Trøndelag Folk Museum are:

• The administration building
• The visitor centre
• Storage magazines at the cellars at the old town

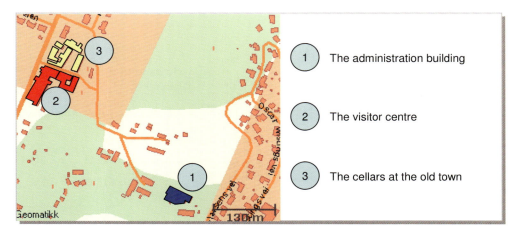

Figure 24: Study building objects at Trøndelag Folk Museum

5.5.1 Study objects

In these case studies the application of the hypoxic air and inert air concepts are evaluated for:

- the whole building,
- multiple rooms and
- single rooms

within these buildings.

The administration building

The administration building was constructed in 2000. It holds both offices, storage magazines, laboratories and workshops, as well as rooms for preparation of exhibitions and artefacts. The storage magazines contain unique collections of books, photos, textiles and wooden items.

Figure 25: The administration building at Sverresborg, Trøndelag Folk Museum

The visitor centre

In the visitor centre there are exhibitions portraying life in the region during the last 150 years "Images of Life" and temporary exhibitions.

This building was constructed in 2000. It holds general public areas, shops, restaurant, offices, storage magazines, laboratories and workshops, rooms for preparation of exhibitions and artefacts, as well as a restaurant area.

In the open-air department there is also a comprehensive ski museum, exhibitions portraying the history of the telephone and telegraph and a kindergarten.

Items of the stored collections are documents, textiles and wooden artefacts.

Figure 26: The visitor centre at Sverresborg, Trøndelag Folk Museum

The cellars at the old town

These buildings, that are wooden houses, are from the old part of downtown Trondheim. Today this is an important part of the visitor area at Sverresborg and parts of the cellars in these houses are used as storage rooms and storage magazines for documents, textiles and wooden items.

Figure 27: The old town at Sverresborg, Trøndelag Folk Museum

5.5.2 The administration building

The method of construction is largely masonry with supplementary wooden details and concrete structures in the basement.

A major part of the areas are supported by mechanical ventilation systems and humidity control systems, with the exception of the storage magazines. There is no information available describing the current infiltration conditions. However, both the observed construction details and the applied constructions products and installations should give relative low infiltration. The building is relative homogenous. The storage magazines that are located in the basement have little infiltration.

The different areas of the building are well separated both physical and technical. Based on this it will be relative easy to establish different air conditions in the different areas with different constraints related to occupancy type and time in hours per day.

In table 9 the different areas are described with occupancy type and time in hours per day. The suggested hypoxic environment oxygen content and technical solution are shown in table 10.

Table 9 Building areas

Area	Occupancy type	Occupancy time in hours per day
Offices	Non-public	8
Preparation rooms	Non-public	8
Technical and service rooms (e.g. toilets)	Non-public	0.5
Storage rooms	Non-public	0.5
Storage magazines	Non-public	1

Table 10 Recommended hypoxic air solution

Area	Acceptable hypoxic air (health)	Recommended hypoxic environment	Technical solution
Offices	15.5-17.4 %	16 %*	Linked to ventilation system/ Single, separate hypoxic air system
Preparation rooms	15.5-17.4 %	16 %*	Linked to ventilation system/ Separate hypoxic air system
Technical and service rooms (e.g. toilets)	13-15 %	15 %*	Linked to ventilation system/ Separate hypoxic air system
Storage rooms	13-15 %	15 %*	Separate hypoxic air system
Storage Storage magazines	15.5-17.4 %	16 %*	Separate hypoxic air system

To be defined in detailed design

All areas in this building, excepting from the storage magazines, are supported with complete ventilation and humidity control systems. A rational and technical well designed solution of a hypoxic air system in this building, as described in table 10, will reduce both the probability of fire and the consequences of any fire in the whole building. To reduce the investment and energy costs the hypoxic air system should not be linked to the existing ventilation system. The best solution here seems to be a single system serving only the storage magazines applying energy recycling solutions. It might also be worth protecting the preparations rooms by the system, but this depends on the complexity and costs of such a solution. When taking the acceptable hypoxic environment into consideration, this should not give any health impact to employees or visitors. There might be a risk of leakage of hypoxic air to the rest of the building both direct and through the energy recycling unit. The hypoxic air will also reduce the degradation of the building structures and the collections, as well as the risk of impacts due to technical errors on water-based fire fighting systems.

A possible solution for the installation is shown in figure 28. Initially we propose that the magazines/library be protected by a hypoxic air system as these areas contain the most important collections and are seldom occupied by the staff. In this case the various areas can be supported by a single system.

As the library area may be occupied by staff or visiting researchers for prolonged periods, working up to 8 hours a day in the room, one can either increase the oxygen concentration during working hours for the whole area or for the library area only. The library area is supported by a current ventilation system that may by used to control the oxygen concentration.

The rest of the areas in this building are used daily by the staff up to 8 hours a day. Due to the requirements in the Norwegian building code, areas that are regularly occupied are required to provide 12 exchanges of air per day. This will result in a fairly high energy consumption.

The administration building

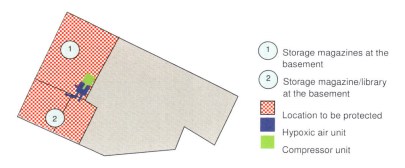

Figure 28: Possible location of the hypoxic air system at the administration building

We estimate the total volume of magazines and library to 1300 m^3. With 1 air exchange per day this gives an energy-consumption of 5.4 kW, and 65 kW with 12 air exchanges per day. This is gross energy-consumption. However, when designing the installations one should carefully consider the possibilities of energy recycling.

5.5.3 The visitor centre

The visitor centre is mainly constructed of brick stone with supplementary wooden details and concrete in the basement floors and walls.

All areas within the building are supported by mechanical ventilation systems and humidity control systems. There is no information available describing the current infiltration conditions. However, both the observed construction details and the applied construction products and installations should give relative low infiltration. The building is relatively homogenous.

The storage magazines that are located in the basement have little infiltration.

The different areas of the building are well separated both physically and technically. Based on this it will be relative easy to establish different air conditions in the different areas with different constraints related to occupancy type and time in hours per day.

In table 11 the different areas are described with occupancy type and time in hours per day. The suggested hypoxic environment oxygen content and technical solution are shown in table 12.

Table 11 Building areas

Area	Occupancy type	Occupancy time in hours per day
Public rooms e.g. restaurants, exhibition areas and general public area	Public	4
Offices	Non-public	8
Preparation rooms	Non-public	8
Technical/service rooms (e.g. toilets)	Non-public	0,5
Storage rooms	Non-public	0,5
Storage magazines	Non-public	1

Table 12 Recommended hypoxic air solution

Area	Acceptable hypoxic air (health)	Recommended hypoxic environment	Technical solution
Public rooms e.g. restaurants, exhibition areas and general public area	15.5-17.4 %	16 %*	Linked to ventilation system/ Single, separate hypoxic air system
Offices	15.5-17.4 %	16 %*	Linked to ventilation system/ Single, separate hypoxic air system
Preparation rooms	15.5-17.4 %	16 %*	Linked to ventilation system/ Separate hypoxic air system
Technical and service rooms (e.g. toilets)	13-15 %	15 %*	Linked to ventilation system/ Separate hypoxic air system
Storage rooms	13-15 %	15 %*	Separate hypoxic air system
Storage magazines	15.5-17.4 %	16 %*	Separate hypoxic air system

* To be defined in detailed design

This building is visited by larger groups of visitors especially during the summer season but also frequently during the rest of the year as it holds a restaurant area. The rooms in the basement are used for storage of different artefacts. Both the storage magazines and the public areas are well separated. One should also expect low infiltration and air leakage in this building. Most of the spaces in the building are also supported with a new ventilation and humidity control system. This gives a potential for rational installation of a hypoxic air system applying energy recycling units with minor technical and economical implications. With the suggested hypoxic environment this should not give any health impact to employees or visitors. However, the probability of fire and the consequences of any fire in the whole building will be reduced as well as the degradation of the building structures and the collections.

The proposed solution as shown in figure 29 and figure 30 will provide the whole building with hypoxic air. As most areas in the building are supported with ventilation and humidity control system, this will simplify the distribution and control of the air. For energy efficiency, there is potential to recycle heat generated by the compressor units for use in the air conditioning unit. To optimize the installation several subsystems may be considered. During summertime one may opt to increase oxygen concentration in the public areas during visiting hours.

First floor

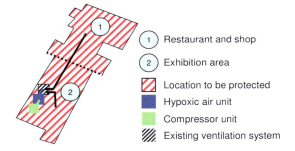

Figure 29: Possible location of the hypoxic air system at the Visitor Centre at first floor

Ground floor

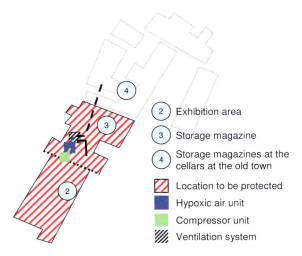

Figure 30: Possible location of the hypoxic air system at the Visitor Centre at ground floor

We estimate the volume of this building to be 1500 m³. 1 air exchange per day makes for a power-demand of 6.3 kW, and 75 kW at 12 air exchanges per day. This is gross energy-consumption. However, when designing the installations one should carefully consider the possibilities of energy recycling.

5.5.4 The cellars at the old town

The buildings in "the old town" are old wooden houses with basement structures made by massive natural stone.

Both the buildings as such and the basements have high infiltration. There are installed humidity control systems in the storage magazines in the cellars. Except for this there are no ventilation systems.

Due to the high infiltration/air leakage these areas will need a high volume of hypoxic air per square metre.

The areas of the building are relatively open spaces, both physically and technically and it may not be easy to establish consistent air conditions in the various areas.

In table 13 the different areas are described with occupancy type and time in hours per day. The suggested hypoxic environment oxygen content and technical solution are shown in table 14.

Table 13 Building areas

Area	Occupancy type	Occupancy time in hours per day
Preparation rooms	Non-public	8
Technical/service rooms (e.g. toilets)	Non-public	0.5
Storage rooms	Non-public	0.5
Storage magazines	Non-public	1

Table 14: Recommended hypoxic air solution

Area	Acceptable hypoxic air (health)	Recommended hypoxic environment	Technical solution
Preparation rooms	15.5-17.4 %	16 %*	Linked to ventilation system/ Separate hypoxic air system
Technical and service rooms (e.g. toilets)	13-15 %	15 %*	Linked to ventilation system/ Separate hypoxic air system
Storage rooms	13-15 %	15 %*	Separate hypoxic air system
Storage magazines	15.5-17.4 %	16 %*	Separate hypoxic air system

* To be defined in detailed design

The cellars at the old town are not occupied by employees or visitors for long periods. However, they will need relative large volumes of hypoxic air to maintain stable conditions due to the expected high infiltration and air leakage. The air leakage to the rest of the building from the basement might also create a hypoxic situation in the whole buildings. The potential and consequences of this depends largely on the frequency of visitors and the infiltration conditions in these buildings. With the proposed solution, as described in table 14, the probability of fire and the consequences of any fire in the buildings will be reduced. The suggested hypoxic environment should not give any health impact to employees or visitors.

As these areas are located close to the visitor centre they can be supported both from the visitor centre and from a local system.

In figure 31 we have outlined a solution with a local system. Even if one selects this solution it might be a good idea to enable parallel support from the visitor centre to increase reliability. These areas are used as storage rooms only and can be protected with as low as 13% oxygen as they are not visited by visitors and seldom by the staff. This also reduces the required air exchange rate. These are however old buildings with high infiltration and in this case it is likely that the infiltration rate becomes the decisive factor.

We estimate the total volume of the protected areas of this building to be 1200 m^3. 1 air change per day makes a power-demand of 5 kW, and 60 kW at 12 air exchanges per day. This is gross energy-consumption. However, when designing the installations one should carefully consider the possibilities of energy recycling. The infiltration is significantly reduced by simple measures at low cost.

The cellars at the old town

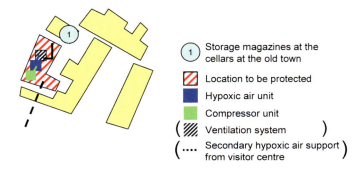

Figure 31: Possible location of the hypoxic air system at the cellars of the old town

6   CONCLUSIONS

Inert (hypoxic) air venting is found to be remarkably promising for heritage appli-cations. Inert air prevents ignition, initial smoke and fire spread. Storage rooms, laboratories and exhibitions may be protected, ranging in size from small closets to large volumes. If applied to public areas, the health concerns for a minority of the population might be dealt with by controlling access to prevent individuals with predispositions for disease in hypoxic air, from entering the protected area. This principle is already established in commercial aviation where similar environ-mental conditions are maintained in aircraft cabins.

Inert air venting equipment may be connected to air conditioning systems or be installed as stand alone systems. In either case, pipes, nozzles or any equipment in the protected rooms are not required for inert air venting. Room fans, sensors and detectors in the protected rooms and activation systems are also not required. The inert air is continuously generated on site, thus a minimum of space is required and no reservoirs run empty or require refilling, in comparison to gas extinguishing systems. Yet another feature of inert air venting makes it uniquely safe: There are no dangerous gases stored which may accidentally be released and threathen life safety. Even if inert air generators produce too much inert air, or premixed inert air reservoirs are emptied unintentionally, the protected rooms are still perfectly safe for normal occupation, evacuation or rescue.

There is virtually no risk of secondary damage, environmental or corrosive issues. As an additional benefit, inert air positively contribute to the diminishing of normal deterioration of organic and non organic objects as well as décor.

A challenge of implementing inert air systems is to optimize energy cost, which depends strongly on air exchange rate and air leakage. Compressors must be lo-cated or encapsulated to reduce noise. Analysis must be done to ensure that any special substance which may burn at a low oxygen level is dealt with by other measures (as with any inert gas extinguishing system) or by incorporating an inert air suppression mode option.

Some national code limits on oxygen level for confined enclosures in buildings may require special permits or management measures such as control of staff or public areas to prevent access by individuals predisposed for heart disease and so on.

In order to optimize inert air venting in the future, research should be done to fur-ther determine fire heat and smoke retarding effects, or damage per minute rates in hypoxic air. Also, effects on smouldering fires should be investigated. Once clari-fied, there is a probability that the oxygen level could be increased in some heritage applications.

The hypotheses presented in section 1.3 have been confirmed by this report's con-tent. They are restated here with some additional observation notes:

STATEMENT OF HYPOTHESIS	CONCLUSION

Benefits of inert air systems

1	Prevents ignition *(in contrast to gas extinguishing systems)*	**Yes** Retards smouldering combustion as well
2	Prevents smoke release prior to fire extinguishing (in contrast to gas extinguishing systems)	**Yes**
3	Prevents backdraught *(in contrast to gas extinguishing systems)*	**Yes** The limited concentration holding time of *extinguishing gas* systems allow for reignition or smouldering: may cause backdraught
4	Fully benign to environment *(in contrast to halon and other gas extinguishing systems)*	**Yes**
5	Not toxic, no residue, no added risk of corrosion	**Yes**
6	Allows considerable room air leakage *(in contrast to gas extinguishing systems)*	**Yes** Energy costs prohibit large leakage application however.
7	Allows open doors for rescue of artefacts, manual intervention, evacuation *(in contrast to gas extinguishing systems)*	**Yes**
8	Do not have limited extinguishant reservoirs *(in contrast to gas extinguishing systems)*	**Yes**
9	No refilling, transport or resetting issues following incidents	**Yes**
10	Applicable to small vital rooms and vaults	**Yes**
11	Applicable to very large room volumes *(galleries or multi-storey, multi-room historic buildings)*	**Yes**
12	Applicable to moderately leaky historic rooms where fixed permanent seals are not acceptable	**Yes** Energy consumption prevents economical applications if very leaky. Imminent next generation membrane separators are expected to be more energy-efficient.
13	Applicable to protection of artefacts which are extremely sensitive to smoke, particles, water, corrosive gas or mechanical impact	**Yes**
14	The inherent simplicity promises high reliability.	**Yes**
15	No installation of nozzles, pipes etc in protected room (when inert air generators are integrated in new or existing air conditioning systems)	**Yes** Nitrogen feed systems require greater complexity in control systems.

Challenges posed by inert air systems

A	Health risk for predisposed individuals in *public* spaces	**Yes** Yet, inert air public applications found acceptable when visitors are inform-ed and access controlled as for entering aircrafts.
B	Some fuels in special spaces like laboratories may require suppression mode and evacuation.	**Yes**
C	Secondary effects of continuous high concentration of nitrogen on fungus or other biological processes thriving by nitrogen.	**No evidence** No substantial research to neither support nor discount.
D	Nitrogen feed systems may cause uneven oxygen levels and require more complex systems to ensure inert air mix, especially in multi-room applications.	**Yes**
E	Power consumption may cause high energy costs.	**Yes** Especially if room is very leaky in the normal state. Imminent next generation membrane separators are expected to be more energy-efficient.

The inherent simplicity of inert air venting promises very high reliability compared to most active fire protection systems.

It is shown that inert air venting offers good potential to avoid invasive installations. Both for single room and multiple room protection various designs of minimal physical or aesthetical intrusion is possible and interventions may be reversible.

The literature studied and referred to about the effects of hypoxic air on artefacts indicates that an hypoxic air environment in a historic building or in a museum store or vault may positively contribute to the diminishing of normal deterioration of organic and non organic objects as well as interior decorations in historic buildings.

If any "health knowledge gap" issue exists about hypoxic air, it is as much about health increase, as it is about health hazards, to occupants.

The main challenge appears to be running costs due to the energy consumption in applications which require high air exchange rate or have a high leakage rate. Careful engineering of hypoxic air units and the way they fit to the air conditioning system may compensate. Both hypoxic air generators and nitrogen generators are relatively new technologies in mass production, and more efficient units are expected. Where location specific analyses are performed to review air exchange rates it may be demonstrated that reduced rates can be satisfactorily adopted rather than observing general "loose fit" industry recommendations. Such an approach could allow energy savings.

A potential challenge is presented by some fuels in specialised spaces like laboratories. Storage rooms appear straightforward to protect.

In contrast to to all other extinguishing media inert air is promising for effective protection during escape from terrorist incidents involving fire or toxic agents in structures. Inert air may also protect museum vaults and exhibitions in similar large scale incidents, and allow for removal and rescue of artefacts.

The feasibility evaluation through the four case studies show that all of the examples may be well protected by properly designed continuous inert air (hypoxic air) systems. The Arezzo Public Library building and the Stenhouse building computer room offer moderate challenges in incorporating the installation. The Linné building and the Arezzo Public Library building seem to offer the most irreplaceable cultural values and should gain the most benefit from inert air systems. The Trøndelag Folk Museum offers the least challenges and lends itself to cost-efficient installation.

REFERENCES

1 Cote, A; Hall J: *National Fire Protection Association Handbook 19th Edition,* Section 2: "Extinguishment with Inert Gases". 2003.

2 Babrauskas, Vytenis, Ph.D: *Ignition Handbook.* Published by Fire Science Publishers, Issaquah. WA, USA. and by the Society of Fire Protection Engineers. ISBN: 0-9728111-3-3. 2003.

3 Dewsbury and Whitely: Hold Time Calculations for Non-Standard Enclosures in *Fire Technology vol. 40 Issue 1,* January 2004.

4 The Society of Fire Protection Engineers and the National Fire Protection Association: *Handbook of Fire Protection Engineering.* 3nd Edition. 2002.

5 The National Fire Protection Association: *Standard 2001: Standard on Clean Agent Fire Extinguishment Systems.* 2004.

6 The National Fire Protection Association Standard 99B: *Standard for Hypobaric Facilities.* 2002.

7 Drysdale, D. D.: *National Fire Protection Association Handbook 19th Edition,* Chapter 2.3: "Chemistry and Physics of Fire". 2003.

8 N.A.

9 Draft International Standard ISO/DIS 19706: *Guidelines for asessing the fire threat to people.* January 2006.

10 *Fire Protection with Low Oxygen or Oxy-reduct Principal Concepts.* Including the *Requirements for Buildings with Permanent Inertisation Concepts.* Allianz. Loss Control Guideline. April 2004 Edition.

11 Brooks, J: *Aircraft Cargo Fire Suppression using Low Pressure Dual Fluid Water Mist and Hypoxic Air.*International Aero Technologies LLC.US.2004.

12 Kotliar, Igor K: *Regulatory and Occupational Health and Safety - Frequently asked Questions (on hypoxic air for fire protection).* Available on request at FirePASS Inc, New York, US. 2004.

13 Berg, P; Lindgren, A: *Fire Prevention and Health Assessment in Hypoxic Environment.* Lund University 2004. Sponsor: Buro Happold Engineers Ltd.

14 *Nitrogen study fertilizes fears of pollution (abstract).* Nature 2005 Feb 24; 433(7028):791.

15 Nowak, Dennis; Angerer, Peter: *Working in permanent hypoxica for fire protection – impact on health (abstract).* Springer-Verlag Heidelberg. 2003.

16 Manufacturer Data Sheets: Kidde-Deugra. *Nitrogen inerting system.* http://www.kidde-deugra.com/en_permasafe.pdf

17 Manufacturer Data Sheets: Innovative Gas Systems Global - Generon. *Nitrogen generators. http://www.igs-global.com/*

18 Manufacturer Data Sheets: Air Products AS. *Nitrogen generators. http://www.airproducts.com/index.asp*

19 Manufacturer Data: Wagner - OxyReduct. *Nitrogen inerting system. http://www.wagner.de/english/*

20 Manufacturer Data: FirePASS. *Hypoxic air venting system. http://firepass.com*

21 Patent Application: Ernst Werner Wagner. WO 9947210. *Fire fighting nitrogen generator for closed room oxygen concentration reduction, to halt combustion.*

22 Patent Application: Werner Wagner. DE 59906865D. *Inertisierungsverfahren zur brandverhütung und -löschung in geschlossenen räumeninertisierungs- verfahren zur brandverhütung und -löschung in geschlossenen räumen.*

23 Patent Application: Ernst Werner Wagner. CZ 20000127. *Internal method of prevention and extiguishing fires in enclosed premises.*

24 Patent Application: Igor K Kotliar.US 6314754B1. *Hypoxic Fire Prevention and Fire Suppression Systems for computer rooms and other human occupied facilities*

25 Patent Application: Igor K Kotliar.US 6334315B1. *Fire Prevention and Fire Sup- pression Systems for computer cabinets and fire-hazardous industrial containers.*

26 Patent Application: Igor K Kotliar. US 6418752. *Hypoxic Fire Prevention and Fire Suppression Systems and Breathable Fire Extinguishing Compositions for Human Occupied Environments.*

27 Patent Application: Igor K Kotliar. US 6401487. *Hypoxic Fire Prevention and Fire Suppression Systems with Breathable Fire Extinguishing Compositions for Human Occupied Environments.*

28 Patent Application: Igor K Kotliar. US 6560991. *Hyperbaric Hypoxic Fire Es- cape And Suppression Systems For Multilevel Buildings, Transportation Tun- nels, And Other Human-Occupied Environments.*

29 Patent Application: Igor K Kotliar. US 6557374. *Tunnel Fire Suppression Sys- tem and Methods for Selective Delivery of Breathable Fire Suppressant Directly To Fire Site.*

30 Patent Application: Igor K Kotliar. US 650242. *Mobile Firefighting Systems with Breathable Hypoxic fire Extinguishing Compositions for Human Occupied Environments.*

31 Phillips K: Little Locust's Breathless Start. *The Journal of Experimental Biol- ogy 207, 386.* 2004 (abstract).

32 Phillips, Kathryn: *The Hypoxic Brain.* The Journal of Experimental Biology 207. 2004 (abstract).

33 Meyer, J R: *Insect Physiology - Respiratory System*. Depart. of Entomology. NC State University. 2001. *http:/www.cals.ncsu.edu/course/ent425/tutorial/respire.html*

34 Kent, P: *Clemson Researcher takes Part in Breakthrough Research on Insects*. Celmson University. Jan 2003. *http://clemsonews.clemson.edu/WWW_releases/2003/January/Insect_Research.html*

35 Insect Breathing Mechanism Discovered. *Pioneering Science and Technology Logos. Spring 2003 – vol 21, no 1*.

36 Researchers Discover Insect Breathing Mechanism. *Museum Information. The Field Museum and Science Daily*. Sources refer *Science* January 2003.

37 Burchill and Billiet: *The Breathing System of Insects – The Tracheal Breathing System of Insects*. The Open Door Web site. *http://www.knockonthedoor.com/*

38 Burmester, T: "A Welcome Shortage of Breath - The respiratory systems of animals must guarantee an efficient oxygen supply. But it seems that, in some insects, they have evolved to restrict the flow of oxygen too". *Nature 433. 2005* (abstract).

39 Hetz and Bradley: "Insects breathe discontinuously to avoid oxygen toxicity". *Nature 433. 2005*.

40 N.A.

41 Krivoshchekov S.G.; Divert G.M.; Divert V.E: "Effect of Short-Term Intermittent Normobaric Hypoxia on the Regulation of External Respiration in Humans" (abstract). *Human Physiology*. ISSN 0362-1197.

42 Maarten Van Der Zwaag: *Oxygen Reduction Systems Promising for Fire Prevention*. Allianz Risk Consultants B.V. 2002 *http://www.allianz.com/azcom/dp/cda/0,,1016833-44,00.html*

43 Andersson, Berggren, Grönkvist, Magnusson, Svensson: *Oxygen saturation and cognitive performance* (abstract). Swedish Defence Research Agency, Division of Command and Control Systems, Department of Man-System Interaction. Psychopharmacology. Springer-Verlag GmbH. 2002.

44 Boman, CarlAxel; Holmberg, Jan; Stymne, Hans: *Monitoring af Air Infiltration in Museums, Case Study: The National Museum of Fine Arts, Stockholm, Sweden*. Pentiaq AB, The Royal Institute of Technology and Univeristy of Gävle, Sweden. 6th Indoor Air Quality Meeting, Padova, 2004.

45 Nord Test Method VVS 118 Approved 1997-11: *Ventilation: Local Mean age of Air – Homogenous Emission Techniques*.

46 Manufacturer Data Sheets: Hypoxico Inc (manufacturer website). *Hypoxic air generators. http://www.hypoxico.com/*

47 *Cargo Compartment alternative MPS testing using Low Pressure dual Fluid Water Mist and Hypoxic Air*. International Aero Inc Fire Protection Laboratory. FAA and JAA. International Aircraft Systems Fire Protection Working Group 2003. Available on request at FirePASS Inc, New York, US.

48 Red Brooks Laboratory/Pyrogen. Website information on hypoxic air for air-craft applications. *http://www.pyrogen.com/IAIfireLab.htm*

49 Iversen, Iver: *Nitrogen Inert Gas Systems based on Membrane Technology.* Unitor ASA. (supplier website) *www.unitor.com*

50 Manufacturer Data: MEDAL/Air Liquide (website). *Nitrogen generators.* *http://www.medal.airliquide.com/en/index.asp*

51 Manufacturer Data: Koatsu Co,Ltd (website). *Nitrogen extinguishing system* *http://www.koatsu.co.jp/pdf/nn100_package_e.pdf*

52 Zwaag van der,Maarten: *Oxygen Reduction Method Promising.*Allianz 2004 *http://www.allianz.com/azcom/dp/cda/0,,1016833-44,00.html*

53 Manufacturer: Lowndesconsult Ltd (website cached, site page removed by pub-lishing date of this report. *FirePASS Applications.*

54 *Hermetic storage: Stepping backwards 3000 years with modern technology.* GrainPro Inc. *http://www.grainpro.com/hermetic.html*

55 Holmberg, Jan G.: "About Risk Assessment of Historic Houses". *Meddelelser 1/2000.Konserveringsnytt.*

References on Effects of Inert Air on Artefacts (section 4.3)

56 Arney, J.S., Jacobs, A.J., Newman, R., "The influence of oxygen on the fading of organic colorants". *Journal of the American Institution for Conservation 18.* 1979.

57 ASHRAE Handbook 2003. HVAC Applications, chapter 21, *Museums, Librar-ies and Archives.* American Society of Heating, Refrigerating and Air-Condi-tioning Engineers, Inc. Atlanta.

58 Bromelle, N.S., 1964."The Russell and Abney Report on the action of light on watercolors". *Studies in Conservation 9(4): 140-51.* London

59 Fielden, B.M.: *Conservation of Historic Buildings.* Architectural Press, Butter-worth-Heineman Ltd. Oxford. 1994.

60 Maekawa S. (Ed.): *Oxygen-Free Museum Cases,* The Getty Conservation Insti-tute (ed. Maekawa, S.) LA. 1998.

61 Thomson G: *The Museum Environment 2nd ed.* Butterworths, London.1986.

62 Riksantikvarieämbetet, 2003. *Syrefria mikroklimat,* Rapport från Riksantikvarieämbetet 2003:3, ed. Fjaestad, M., Åkerlund, M., Bergh, JE.,Stockholm.

References on Health and Safety (section 4.5)

63 AFS 1993:3 - *Arbete i slutet utrymme*, Arbetarskyddsstyrelsen, 1993

63 Angerer, P. et al: *Working in permanent hypoxia for fire protection – impact on health*, Int Arch Occup Environ Health, 76, pp. 87-102. 2003.

64 Aviation Health Working Group: *Study of possible effects on health of aircraft cabin environment – stage 2* (98 pages). 2001.

65 Bartels H., Dejours P, Kellog RH, Mead J: *"Glossary on respiration and gas exchange"*. *Journal of Applied Physiology*. 24 (4): 549-558. 1973.

66 Gustavsson, C. et al: *Effects of normobaric hypoxic confinement on human performance*. Swedish Defence Research Establishment (FOA), Hårsfjärden. 1997.

67 Knight, D.R.; A. Cymerman, J.A. Devine, R.L Burse, C.S Fulco, P.B Rock, D.V. Tappan, A.A.Messier, and H. Carhart: *Symptomatology during hypoxic exposure to flame- retardant chamber atmospheres*. Undersea Biomedical Research. 17 (1):33-44. 1990a.

68 Knight, D.R., C.L. Shlichting, C.S Fulco, and A.Cymerman: *Mental performance during sub maximal exercise in 13 and 17 % oxygen*. Undersea Biomedical Research. 17 (3):223-230. 1990b.

69 Linde, L., C. Gustafsson, and H.Ornhagen: *Effects of reduced oxygen partial pressure on cognitive performance in confined spaces*. Military Psychology 9 (2): 151-168. 1997.

70 N.A.

71 Occupational Safety & Health Administration, *Permit-required confined spaces* - 1910.146, 15th August 2004. *www.osha.gov*

72 Taylor, A.D. and Bronks: "Effects of acute normobaric hypocia on quadriceps integrated electromyogram and blood metabolites during incremental exercise to exhaustion". *European Journal of Applied Occupational Physiology*. 73 (1-2):121-129. 1996.

73 "Emergency and Continuous Exposure Guidance Levels for Selected Submarine Contaminants, Cap11 Oxygen, pp 207-227". *Subcommittee on Emergency and Continuous Exposure Guidance Levels for Selected Submarine Contaminants, Committee on Toxicology, National Research Council 2004*. National Academics Press. 2004.

74 Walford et al: ""Biospheric Medicine" as Viewed From the Two-Year First Closure of Biosphere 2". *Aviation Space Environmental Medicine*; 67:609-17. 1996

76 Rusko, H. R. New aspects of altitude training. The American Journal of Sports Medicine. 24(6):S48-S521996.

77 Baker, A &Hopkins, W.G.1998. Altitude training for sea-level competition. Sportscience Training & Technology. Internet Society for Sport-Science. http://sportsci.org/traintech/altitude/wgh.html.

COMMENTS ON A KEY REFERENCE, BERG ET AL[13]

Fire Prevention and Health Assessment in Hypoxic Environment
(Master Thesis of Berg, Petter; Lindgren, Andreas. Lund University.
Sponsored by Buro Happold).

This thesis report provides a fairly comprehensive overview of inert air for fire protection in general, is available on the internet and can be readily referred to. However, it is a master thesis on risk management, and readers should be aware of the following:

1. Their case study and evaluations are in general based on nitrogen feed inerting to provide hypoxic air, not on hypoxic air venting. The thesis' cautious or negative conclusions are not applicable to hypoxic air *venting*.

2. Ignition properties of materials in hypoxic air are focused on, rather than the more relevant burning properties, fire retarding effects and damage per minute. Also, class B fires (flammable liquid fires) and fires in plastics (these fires ought to be treated as a kind of class B fire in this context) are focused on, treating the latter as A fires. The impact of hypoxic air on typical class A fires (typically materials like wood, paper, textiles) are not dealt with in the report, and the reason for focussing on class B fires is arson. In reality, however, liquid arson fires soon turn into class A fires once liquid is consumed. Hypoxic air retards class A fires efficiently and is superior to inert gases for extinguishing. Hypoxic air efficiently prevents or retards shielded fires better than sprinkler and water mist extinguishing systems. The authors of the thesis do acknowledge the lack of data on hypoxic air effects on class A fires and call for research.

3. Risks to occupants from (smouldering) fire and from hypoxic air are evaluated specifically, whereas comparison to relevant conditions when using conventional inert gases for extinguishing are not made. In some cases, the strict evaluations made in this report would, if applied to extinguishing systems employing pure inert gases, carbon dioxide or gas blends of argon and nitrogen, lead to the application of these gases not being recommended.

4. In the report it is not recognized that all extinguishing systems require intervention to extinguish any residual fire and clear the fire source. Listing residual smouldering fires, or even retarded flaming fires, as both a failure of inert air systems and an unacceptable health risk is erroneous. Portraying 'smoke explosions' or backdraughts (although properly noted as very rare) as a risk to inert air systems is not correct as they also occur in fires inerted by their own smoke and in fires extinguished by inert gas. In fact, we consider smoke explosions might present a greater risk with conventional "one shot" gas extinguishing systems since fires are known to subsequently reignite, rebuild or pose backdraught risks due to leakage and decreased concentration by the time intervening personnel arrive.

5. Proper early smoke detection systems in rooms that justify special fire protection is a prerequisite of all concepts of prevention or extinguishing, and certainly not a necessity relating to inert air systems only, as stated in the thesis.

6. The conclusion that fire gases become more toxic in hypoxic air vented rooms is hardly valid. First, the very purpose of inerting is to prevent fire gases being formed, and second, all fires lower oxygen levels in the room. In any case, no one occupies rooms with smouldering or flaming fires - they evacuate. The risk of any fire smoke far exceeding the theoretical worsening effect of hypoxic air, and the simultaneous retarding effect of hypoxic air on the smoke yield, does not seem to be taken into account in the report.

7. The evaluation of public spaces does not include various inert air system modes. Adoption of temporarily increased, or normal, O_2 concentrations during opening hours, or restricted access to protected spaces similar to predisposed persons not being allowed on air flights, are not considered.

Notwithstanding these observations, the report provides useful introductory information and an overview of many aspects relating to inert air, and we have appreciated and referenced many of the illustrations and valid points made.

APPENDIX B

Published Information by Manufacturers

B1   KNOWN MANUFACTURERS AND LICENSEES

This appendix contains open published information on hypoxic air systems as acquired from the websites of all the product manufacturers and hypoxic air venting licensees as they are known to the authors at time of writing. This list is not to be misconstrued as an endorsement of those. Listed and other companies involved in this field able to provide comparable services may exist.

The list of known players in the hypoxic air industry will undoubtely change rapidly in forthcoming years.

- FirePASS (patent rights)
- Wagner (patent rights, manufacturer of nitrogen feed systems)
- Doll Technology Group (license to manufacture/market hypoxic air systems)
- Lowndesconsult (former hypoxic air venting licensee)
- Fireprev Ltd (vendor of hypoxic air venting systems)
- Kidde-Deugra PermaSafe (licensee/vendor of nitrogen feed systems)
- Air Products (manufacturer of hollow fibre membranes*)
- Generon ICS (manufacturer of hollow fibre membranes*)
- Unitor (vendor of hollow fibre membranes)
- Air Liquide, MEDAL (manufacturer of hollow fibre membranes*)
- Hypoxico (manufactuer of hypoxic air generators)
- Koatsu (manufacturer of nitrogen extinguishing system)

   * *Membranes applied in nitrogen feed hypoxic air systems, nitrogen hypoxic air generators, nitrogen gas inerting systems or general nitogen production).*

The figures and description excerpts are choosen to complement the content of this report in terms of illustrating equipment and providing details of aspects for the benefit of readers. Refer to "References" for source details.

B2 HYPOXIC AIR SYSTEM DESIGNS

Nitrogen Feed Systems (Continuous)

Wagner[19]

OxyReduct by Wagner[19] is referred to as a pioneer nitrogen feed concept in this report. Wagner presents the system as shown in figure B2.1:

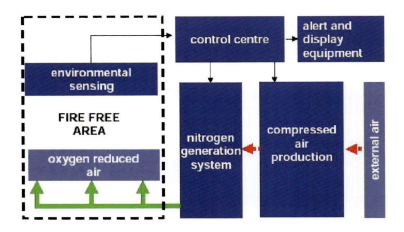

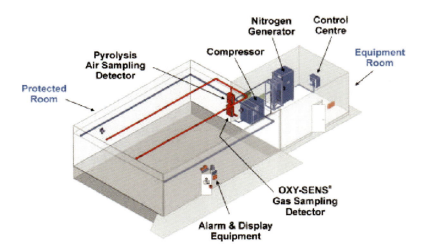

Figure B2.1: Nitrogen generation system by Wagner[19].

During the work on this report attempts were made to contact Wagner for details on the concept. Without success the only information available was accessed from the internet.

The figures and text below are extracts from the internet (not confirmed facts):

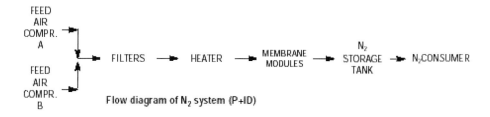

Figure B2.2: Nitrogen feed system[19]

- The UK Health and Safety Executive (HSE, UK) classifies areas of reduced oxygen as confined space, thus require a management system to monitor people access.
- Equipment size depends on leakage rate, not room volume. Space saving possible from 500 m^3 up.
- Pyrolysis can still occur.
- Generator vents air with an enriched oxygen content of 30%.
- Generator must be within 30 m of compressor, but no reasonable distance limit generator to protected volume.
- Steel pipe required between generator and protected volume. Plastic pipe acceptable within volume.
- Pressure at outlet into protected volume negligible.
- Compressor power consumption 5kW to 65 kW depending upon leakage rate.
- Air filters to be renewed once per year.
- Generator membrane life in excess of ten years.

Air Products and Air Liquide MEDAL[18,50]

Plants to produce nitrogen: Air Products and Air Liquide MEDAL are two manu-facturers of nitrogen membrane separators used with nitrogen feed systems.

Figure B2.3: Membrane separators to produce nitrogen on site, Air Products. Paper clip illus-trates size of hollow fibre ends. The nitrogen generator has the capacity of 50 m3/h. Standard shipboard units provide from 15-6250 m3/h at purity of 95-96 N_2. Pressure of compressors vary within 5.5 to 20 barg, depending on purity etc.[18]

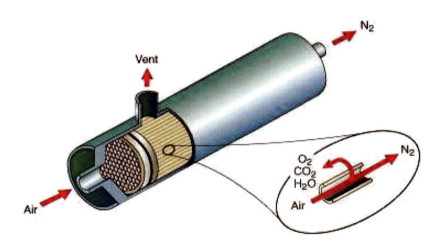

Relative Permeation Rates														
Fast	H_2O	He	H_2	NH_3	CO_2	H_2S	O_2	Ar	CO	N_2	CH_4	C_2H_4	C_3H_6	Slow

Figure B2.4: Hollow fibre membranes, Air Liquide MEDAL[50], to produce nitrogen on site. Gases permeate fibres at different rates.

Hypoxic Air Venting Systems (Continuous)

Figure B2.5 illustrates a generic system design of *preventing* mode of hypoxic air venting (FirePASS[20]).

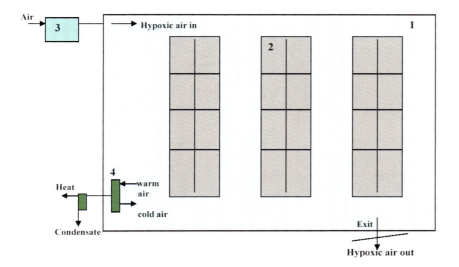

1 – Protected Space room, 2-Storage racks, 3-Hypoxic generator, 4-Split a/c unit

The preventative system illustrated above works as follows:

    a.   Ambient air is drawn into the hypoxic generator where it is purified and made hypoxic.
    b.   The air ventilates the entire room inhibiting any common ignition sources.
    c.   Hypoxic air leaks from the room thus completing the flow and ventilating the facility.
    d.   Heating/ Air-Conditioning units must be split-type closed dedicated systems.

Figure B2.5: Preventative hypoxic air venting: Fire does not ignite, temperature does not rise and the oxygen concentration is constant at, for example, 15%.

Inerting on Demand (Automatic extinguishing using hypoxic air)

Such systems are like ordinary extingushing systems including detectors and actuating mechanisms, except they:

- Contain premixed hypoxic air
- Are refilled on site automatically
- Allow occupation for extended or limited period depending on concentration

The equipment generating the hypoxic air for such applications is same as for continuous systems.

B3 MANUFACTURED PRODUCTS

Hypoxico Inc[46]

Hypoxico Inc is a company considered a world leader in altitude simulation equipment. The workout chambers they provide apply hypoxic air by the same equipment used for hypoxic air fire protection, and their equipment and experience are useful to us in order to evaluate occupation in inert air rooms[46].

Their hypoxic air generators appear fairly simple, yields 6 000 l/h and appear to be tested to keep oxygen concentration quite invariable at continuous operation – 14.82-14.86% over 2 days (comparable to altitude of 1800 m). Such units can be bought for around $ 6.000.

Figure B3.1: A small hypoxic air generator (Hypoxico Inc), as used to provide an oxygen of 14.5% in small fitness training rooms, equivalent to 2800m of altitude. Optional adapters will provide oxygen level as low as 8.5 % equivalent to 6970 m. The generator is 55 cm x 58 cm x 27 cm (21.5" x 23" x 10.5"), weighs 25kg and can be placed in a separate room[20]

The Hypoxico generators are based on the pressure swing adsorption principle. See Appendix B4 for description of principle.

Air Products[18]

Air Products manufacture nitrogen generators for application in ships, based on flue gases or and membrane separators.

8% oxygen is defined by the International Maritime Organisation as inert atmosphere in rooms with *hydrocarbon* fire risks.

Nitrogen is not used for occupational atmospheres, but for blanketing and purging of chemicals and other cargoes for fire prevention. Nitrogen is also used to prevent degradation of cargoes sensitive to oxygen, moisture of combustion by-products. Super-dry nitrogen is ideal as a non-freezing, non-corrosive instrument gas and for drying of void spaces.

Their systems are claimed to provide Nitrogen at between one-tenth and one-half the cost of merchant nitrogen in cylinders.

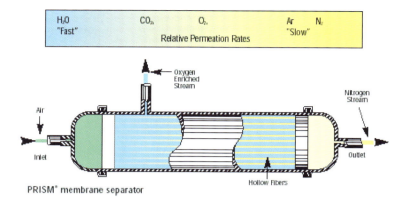

Figure B3.2: *Principle of semi permeable membrane separator to produce nitrogen on site*[18]

Nitrogen flowrate and purity are however inverse parameters, and it is therefore not economical to generate higher purity than is actually needed. It is important to observe this, i.e. nitrogen feed systems which offer 95-99% of nitrogen require higher power consumption than systems for hypoxic air producing 84% nitrogen. The cost of compressor power consumption must be optimized by considering that small high pressure systems may equal larger low pressure systems etc.

Kidde-Deugra PermaSafe[16]
PermaSafe is a product for nitrogen feed to provide hypoxic air, similar to the OxyReduct by Wagner, incorporating sensors in the protected room volume.

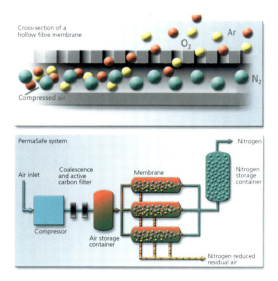

Figure B3.3: *Nitrogen feed system Permasafe*[16]

B4 LARGE NITROGEN GENERATORS

Air Products[18]

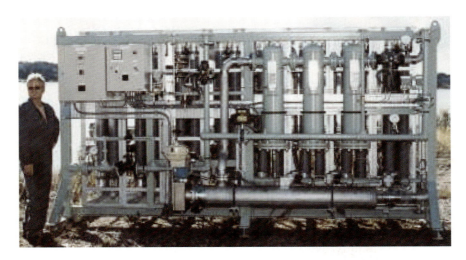

Figure B4.1: Membrane separators to produce nitrogen on site, Air Products. The nitrogen generator has a capacity of 1000 m^3/h. Standard manufactured shipboard unit capacities are 15-6250 m^3/h at purity of 95-96 N_2. Pressure of compressors operates within 5.5 to 20 barg, depending on purity etc[18]

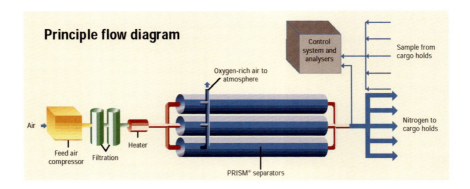

Figure B4.2: Membrane separators to produce nitrogen on site. This illustration shows the principle of system to extend storage life of perishable cargo, purging cargo holds using 95-98 % N_2 - alternatively, nitrogen is delivered by hoses to containers[18]

Generon IGS[17]

Claims highest efficiency membrane. Their units have been in service for more than 13 years (membrane separators in general were introduced into the market 20-30 years ago). Performances: 90-99.9 nitrogen purity, operational within -40 up to 40 degrees Celsius. Unites available for capacities 1.4-274 Nm3/h.

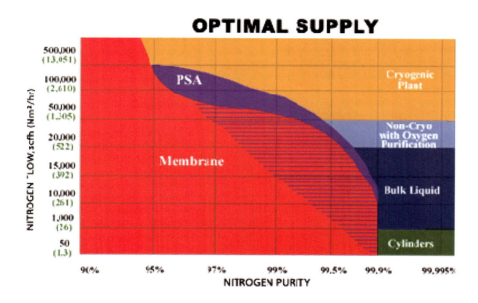

Figure B4.3: Illustration of suitability of various techniques to provide nitrogen at site, made by Generon IGS [17]. For hypoxic air in fire prevention, suppression membrane separators or pressure swing adsorption (PSA) generators are the only ones currently used.

PSA: 0.6 up to 10 000 m3/h. Up to 99.995 %.

PSA is an older technology but still favoured where high purity N_2 is required. Fire protection systems do not require high purity, but for smaller applications PSA may turn out least expensive.

Unitor[49] (Generon IGS)

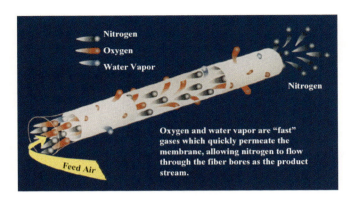

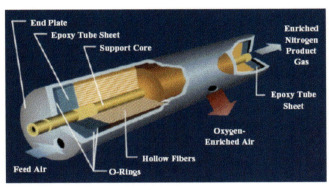

Figure B4.4: Illustrations above [49] describe membrane separators for shipboard applications. They are usually designed for higher N_2 purity than required for fire protection only, and will not be explained in detail. Similar arrangements of equipment may be used with generators for hypoxic air for fire protection purposes.

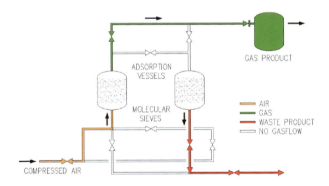

Figure B4.5: The principle of the Pressure Swing Adsorption (PSA)technology is based on air separated in a bed using a carbon molecular sieve where the oxygen molecules are adsorbed much faster than the nitrogen molecules. When the carbon bed is pressurized the gas flowing out will be pure nitrogen. However, the carbon bed will become saturated with oxygen in about one minute, and has to be depressurised and purged by a nitrogen product to remove the oxygen. Duplicte carbon beds are used in the system so that at the same time a second carbon bed is pressurised to maintain a continuous nitrogen flow. A complete PSA system will include a feed air compressor (preferably dry/oil free), an air receiver to equalise the swinging air requirement, a refrigerated dryer, filter system, two carbon bed towers and a nitrogen receiver to equalise the nitrogen purity. For these systems the quality and the timing and control of the automatic valve operation of the in let and outlet valves of the carbon beds is very critical to maintain the high purity of nitrogen.